WILD of
WASHINGTON
and OREGON

T. Abe Lloyd
Fiona Hamersley Chambers

LONE
PINE

Lone Pine Publishing International

© 2014 by Lone Pine Publishing International
First printed in 2014   10 9 8 7 6 5 4 3 2 1
Printed in China

The Distributor: Lone Pine Publishing
1808 B Street NW, Suite 140
Auburn, WA 98001 USA
Website: www.lonepinepublishing.com

Publisher's Cataloging-In-Publication Data
(Prepared by The Donohue Group, Inc.)

Lloyd, T. Abe, author.
    Wild berries of Washington and Oregon / T. Abe Lloyd, Fiona Hamersley Chambers.

    pages : illustrations (some colored), map ; cm

Includes bibliographical references and index.
ISBN: 978-976-650-057-3

      1. Berries—Washington (State)—Identification. 2. Berries—Oregon—Identification. I. Hamersley Chambers, Fiona, 1970– , author. II. Title.

QK144 .L56 2014   581.4/6409795

Editorial Director: Nancy Foulds
Project Editor: Nicholle Carrière
Production Manager: Leslie Hung
Layout & Production: Alesha Braitenbach
Map: Volker Bodegom
Cover Design: Gerry Dotto
Cover and title page images: © Thinkstock 2010

DISCLAIMER: This guide is not meant to be a "how-to" reference guide for consuming wild berries. We do not recommend experimentation by readers, and we caution that many of the plants in Washington and Oregon, including some berries, are poisonous and harmful. The authors and publisher are not responsible for the actions of the reader.

PC: 25

Dedication

To Katrina, whose berry-stained fingers I firmly clasp as we forage the sunny trail, this book is lovingly dedicated.

–T. Abe Lloyd

To my sons, Hayden and Ben, who are the very best berry pickers and tasters I know. Gathering wild foods together gives us such delicious joy and lasting memories, and has connected us to the coastal landscape we are so fortunate to call home. I hope this book will enable other parents to share this experience and tradition of stewardship with their families, too. I would also like to acknowledge those teachers and mentors who I have been privileged to learn from and to the First Nations, botanists and settlers who kept written records or oral accounts of traditional berry use and management. I am particularly indebted to Dr. Nancy Turner for her phenomenal knowledge, mentorship and friendship over many decades.

–Fiona Hamersley Chambers

Acknowledgments

I am deeply indebted to the many photographers who generously contributed such fine images, especially my former Northland College "roomie" Keir Morse and Washington Native Plant Society colleague Mark Turner. Without their excellent photographs, this book would not have been possible.

A huge thanks to my friend Fiona Hamersley Chambers, who pitched this project to me and whose book *Wild Berries of British Columbia* formed the backbone for this one. Thanks also to Lone Pine editor Nicholle Carrière for her optimism, kindness and diligence.

Most importantly, I would like to acknowledge the Native Americans, explorers, naturalists, mentors and friends whose legacies of plant knowledge about our wonderful region they have shared with me and others through their teachings, writings and stories. My deepest appreciation goes out to Dr. Nancy Turner for her vast scholarship and warm mentorship, and to Sam Thayer for his inspiring life example and enduring friendship.

–T. Abe Lloyd

CONTENTS

THE BERRIES

LIST OF RECIPES

Plants at a Glance

TREES AND SHRUBS

Pacific Crab Apple p. 28

Madrona p. 32

Junipers p. 34

Hawthorns p. 40

Mountain-ashes p. 44

Wild Roses p. 48

Red Cherries p. 54

Chokecherry p. 60

Plums p. 64

Indian-plum p. 68

Smooth Sumac p. 70

Blackberries p. 72

Raspberries p. 78

Thimbleberry p. 84

Salmonberry p. 86

Oregon-grapes p. 88

Currants p. 92

Gooseberries p. 98

Prickly Currants p. 104

Serviceberries p. 106

Dogwoods p. 110

Bunchberry p. 114

Huckleberries p. 116

Blueberries p. 122

Cranberries p. 128

False-wintergreens p. 132

Salal p. 136

Bearberries & Manzanitas p. 138

Black Crowberry p. 144

White Mulberry p. 146

Netleaf Hackberry p. 148

Elderberries p. 150

Bush-cranberries & Viburnums p. 154

Honeysuckles p. 160

Soapberry p. 164

Silverberry p. 166

Silktassels p. 168

Oregon Myrtle p. 170

California Wild Grape p. 172

HERBACEOUS PLANTS

One-flowered Clintonia p. 174

Twisted-stalks p. 176

False Lily-of-the-Valley p. 180

False Solomon's-seals p. 182

Fairybells p. 184

Strawberries p. 186

Brittle Prickly Pear p. 190

Groundcherries &
Wild Tomatoes p. 192

Nightshades p. 196

Wolfberry p. 202

California Greenbriar
p. 204

Spikenards p. 206

Bastard Toadflax p. 208

POISONOUS BERRIES

Cascara, Buckthorn, Redberry & Coffeeberry p. 210

English Holly p. 214

Pacific Yew p. 216

Black Twinberry p. 218

Poison-ivy & Poison-oak
p. 220

Devil's Club p. 222

Snowberries p. 224

Climbing Nightshade p. 228

Belladonna p. 230

Coastal Manroot p. 232

Red Baneberry p. 234

Pokeweed p. 236

Spurgelaurel p. 238

Mistletoes &
Dwarf Mistletoes p. 240

Privet p. 244

Map of Washington and Oregon

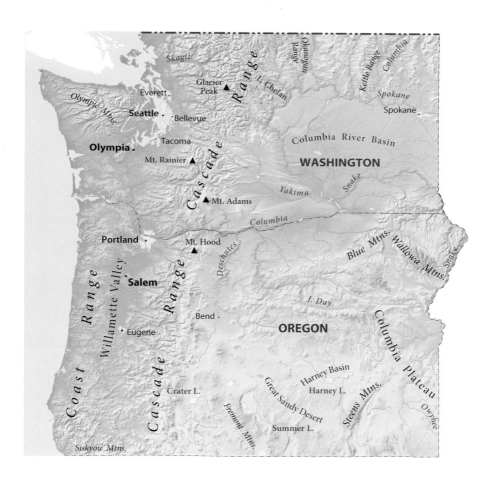

Introduction

Woodland strawberry (*Fragaria vesca*)

It's difficult to find someone who does not enjoy eating berries. Juicy, sweet, tart, sometimes sour, bursting with flavor and very good for you— wild berries are gifts from the land, treasures to be discovered on a casual hike or potentially a lifesaving food if you're unfortunate enough to get lost in the woods. Berries have a long history of human use and enjoyment as food and medicine, in ceremonies and for ornamental and wildlife value. Our ancestors needed to know as a matter of survival which berries were edible or poisonous, where they grew and in which seasons and how to preserve them for non-seasonal use. These early

peoples often went to great lengths to manage their wild berry resources: pruning, coppicing, burning, transplanting and even selectively breeding some wild species into the domesticated ancestors of many of our modern fruit varieties.

Today, many of us live in urban environments where the food on our plate and in our pantries comes from great distances away. The first strawberry is no longer an eagerly awaited and delectable harbinger of the summer to come. Rather than a fleetingly sweet June moment, these fruits are now available on our grocery store shelves almost year-round. A sad result of this convenience and lack of seasonality is that this store-bought fruit has little resemblance to its forebears. Grocery store strawberries, for example, are generally not properly ripe, don't have much flavor and are not loaded with nutrients. As we become more and more disconnected from our food sources, it is even possible that we are forgetting what a "real" berry tastes like. Perhaps part of the exceptional taste of wild fruit is the thrill of the hunt and the discovery of a gleaming berry treasure hanging—sometimes in great profusion—from a vine or bush. These wild berries are only available for a short time during the year, and we must increasingly travel to find them growing in their native state. We must make an effort to discover them in the wild or find a reputable source for those plants that will grow in our home gardens.

The wild berries described in this book are, for the most part, not available in stores. When they are, they are often very expensive. A berry in its prime state of ripeness is juicy and delicate, and therefore does not travel well. What a pity, as slowly savoring one of these fruits at its peak of perfection plucked fresh off the plant is one of the great joys in life. What better way to spend a warm summer's day than wandering hillsides, country roads or forest edges with friends and family in search of these delectable morsels? Wild berry gathering builds community and family and is a great way to connect you and your children to nature. In winter, a spoonful of these frozen or preserved wild fruits will bring back the taste of summer for a delicious moment. Whether you are a seasoned gatherer or a new enthusiast, this book will help guide you to experience and share in this wonderful and generous gift of nature.

Why Learn to Identify and Gather Wild Berries?

Berries gathered in the wild generally have superb flavor and can be picked when they are properly ripe. These fruits are not only delicious, but contain important nutrients and phytochemicals (such as anti-cancer compounds) that are increasingly lacking from our commercially available fruits. Many wild berries are high in vitamin C and also contain trace elements, carbohydrates, proteins and important nutrients such as iron, calcium, thiamine and vitamin A. While most people will obtain this guidebook in order to enjoy wild berries on hikes and outings, the

Wild red raspberry (*Rubus idaeus*)

information that you learn here could also save your life if you ever get stranded or lost in the backcountry. Be warned, though! Gathering wild berries can also be considered a dangerous "gateway" into the more complex realm of preserving and cooking with these fruits, as well as growing them in your own backyard. Once you start on this journey it can become rather addictive and even spread to friends and family!

What Is Not Covered in this Guide?

Although this book should enable you to identify nearly all the native and escaped ornamental berry species in your region, it is not intended as a complete reference guide. A section on references and further reading is provided for those wishing to study these plants in greater detail. Some berry species are so rarely found or have such a restricted range that it would not be useful to include them here. There are many excellent resources already available to help you understand the cultivation and use of domesticated fruit species, so these are also not covered. Nuts, seeds and cones are not considered "berries" in the common sense of the word, so these are excluded.

What Is a "Berry"?

In this guide, "berry" is used in the popular sense of the word, rather than in strictly botanical terms, and includes any small, fleshy fruit. Technically, a "berry" is a fleshy, simple

fruit produced from a single ovary that contains one or more ovule-bearing structures (carpels), each of which has one or more seeds. The outside covering (endocarp) of a berry is generally soft, moist and fleshy, most often in a globular shape. Roughly translated, a berry is really a seed or seeds packaged in a tasty, moist pulp that encourages animals to eat the fruit and distribute the seeds far and wide from the parent plant so that these offspring can grow and flourish. "True berries" include currants, huckleberries, blueberries and grapes.

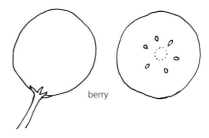

berry

Botanically, however, what we call a "berry" often includes simple, fleshy fruits such as drupes and pomes. The botanical definitions of these different types of fruit are provided below for general interest and are also sometimes mentioned, where appropriate, in the text.

A "drupe" is a fleshy stone fruit that closely resembles a berry but has a single seed or stone with a hard

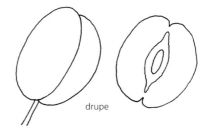

drupe

Himalayan blackberry (*Rubus armeniacus*)

inner ovary wall that is surrounded by fleshy tissue. Wild fruit in this category includes highbush cranberries and bunchberries; some domestic fruit examples are cherries or plums.

A "compound drupe" or "aggregate" fruit ripens from a flower that has multiple pistils, all of which ripen together into a mass of multiple fruits called "drupelets." Drupelets are tiny fruits that form within the same flower from individual ovaries. As a result, these fruits are often crunchy and seedy. Wild examples include raspberries and blackberries. Cultivated examples include tayberries, loganberries and boysenberries.

A "multiple fruit" is similar to an aggregate but differs in that it ripens

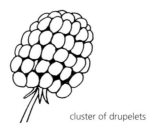

cluster of drupelets

from a number of separate flowers that grow closely together, each with its own pistil (as opposed to from a single flower with many pistils). Mulberry is a native example of a multiple fruit. Tropical examples include pineapples and figs.

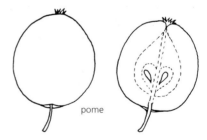

pome

An "accessory fruit" is a simple fruit with some of its flesh deriving from a part other than the ripened ovary. In other words, a source other than the ovary generates the edible part of the fruit. Other names for this type of fruit include pseudocarp, false fruit or spurious fruit. A "pome" is a sort of accessory fruit because it has a fleshy outer layer surrounding a core of seeds enclosed with bony or cartilage-like membranes (it is this inner core that is considered the "true" fruit). Serviceberries and hawthorns are wild examples of pomes; apples and pears are domestic examples. Another type of accessory fruit is the strawberry; the main part of the fruit derives from the receptacle (the fleshy part that stays on the plant when you pick a raspberry) rather than from the ovary. Wintergreen is also an example of an accessory fruit type because the fruit is really a dry capsule surrounded by a fleshy calyx.

A "cone" is a fruit that is made up of scales (sporophylls) that are arranged in a spiral or overlapping pattern around a central core, and in which the seeds develop between the scales. The juniper is an example of a species that produces cones.

cone

A "hip" has a collection of bony seeds (achenes), each of which comes from a single pistil, covered by a fleshy receptacle that is contracted at the mouth. The rose hip (which is also an accessory fruit) is our only example of a hip.

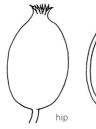

hip

The Species Accounts

In this book, species are organized by growth form into three main sections—**Trees & Shrubs, Herbaceous Plants** and **Poisonous Plants**. Closely related or similar plants are grouped together for comparison, and the section on poisonous plants is conveniently located at the end of the book.

This book includes nearly all the plants that produce fleshy fruit in Washington and Oregon that can be found growing in the wild. Many of these fruits have been used by people both in ancient times and in the present. Each account has a detailed description for the featured species, including plant form, leaf structure, habitat and range, as well as fruit form, color and season. This description, in addition to color photographs and illustrations,

English hawthorn (*Crataegus monogyna*)

Bunchberry (*Cornus canadensis*)

will help you ensure safe plant and berry identification. Information on traditional and contemporary uses for food, medicines and material culture are also included for general interest.

Information is presented in an easy-to-follow format. In addition to the opening general discussion, each species account includes subheadings of **Edibility** (see below for edibility scale), **Fruit** (a description of the look and taste of the fruit), **Season** (flowering and fruiting seasons) and **Description** (a detailed description of the plant, flowers, habitat and range).

Many species accounts focus on a single species, but if several similar species have been used in the same ways, two or more species may be described together. In these "group" accounts, you will find a general description for the group, but there will also be separate paragraphs in which the individual species are described in specific detail. So, for example, the Hawthorns (*Crataegus*

spp.) account describes historical and modern uses in the opening discussion, then has subheadings of Edibility, Fruit, Season and Description for all hawthorns. These subheadings are followed by separate paragraphs with important specific information (including identification and location details) for each of the numerous hawthorns in the region (black hawthorn, English hawthorn, fireberry hawthorn, Suksdorf's hawthorn).

Where appropriate, you will find an **Also called** subheading that describes other common and scientific names for each species. These other names can be found below the title main of the account and at the end of individual species description paragraphs inside the account.

Edibility Scale

All accounts contain a useful scale of edibility for each species. Although we have a wonderful variety of native

15

berries, it is useful to know which ones are worth our time pursuing, which ones, although considered "edible," are better left for the birds or as a famine food and which ones are toxic or poisonous.

Highly edible describes those berries that are most delicious and are well worth gathering and consuming. A wild strawberry or serviceberry is considered highly edible.

Edible describes those berries that are tasty but not as good as the highly edible species. Bunchberry is an example of such a fruit.

Not palatable describes berries you can eat without any ill effects but are perhaps not worth the effort to harvest given their lack of flavor, bitterness, relatively large seeds or lack of fleshiness. It is useful to know about these species in case you are desperate to snack on something in the woods, but they are not berries that you would actively gather to make a pie! Silverberry is an example of such a species.

Devil's club (*Oplopanax horridus*)

Edible with caution (toxic) are berries that are palatable, but have differing reports as to their edibility, or perhaps they are only toxic if you eat large amounts or if they haven't been prepared properly or are unripe. Berries of our native juniper species are an example under this category.

Poisonous berries are ones that are definitely toxic and should not be eaten. An example of a poisonous berry is devil's club.

Season

The season given for flowering and fruit production for each species is an average. Specific microclimates such as deep valley bottoms or high mountaintops will necessarily produce a wide range of flowering and fruiting variability for the same plant. Berry plants also produce fruit of differing quality and quantity from year to year, depending on factors such as plant age and health, changes in temperature and moisture, or insect infestation. Some berries, such as rose hips, are best harvested later in the year after the first frost sweetens the fruit.

Description

The plant description and the accompanying photos and illustrations are important parts of each species account. Each plant description begins with a general outline of the form of the species or genus named at the top of the page. Detailed information about diagnostic features of the leaves, flowers and fruits is then provided. Flowering time is often included as part of the

Prairie rose (*Rosa woodsii*)

flower description to give some idea of when to look for blooms, and a general fruiting season is also included. If two or more species of the same genus have been used for similar purposes, several of the most common species may be illustrated and their distinguishing features described.

Plant characteristics such as size, shape, fruiting, color and hairiness vary with season and habitat and with the genetic variability of each species. Identification can be especially tricky when plants have not yet flowered or fruited. If you are familiar with a species and know its leaves or roots at a glance, you may be able to identify it at any time of year (from very young shoots to the dried remains of last year's plants), but sometimes, positive identification is just not possible.

General habitat information is provided for each species to give you some idea of where to look for a plant. The habitat description provides information about general habitat (e.g., in moist, mossy forests), elevation (e.g., low to montane elevations) and range (e.g., from the northern part of a state to its southern regions). The species ranges and habitats described in this guide were obtained from *Flora of North America*, the United States Department of Agriculture PLANTS Database website, regional field guides, personal experience and interviews, academic papers and other sources. Despite all due diligence being taken, however, this description is not universal or foolproof. Plants sometimes either grow outside their reported ranges or cannot be found within the described habitat. The habitat information included for each species is meant as a general guide only; plants often grow in a variety of habitats over a broad geographical range.

The origin of non–North American species is also noted. The flora of many areas has changed dramatically over the past 200 years, especially in and around human settlements. European settlers brought many plants with them, either accidentally (in ship ballast, packing and livestock bedding) or purposely (for food, medicine, fiber or ornamental value). Some of these introduced species produce fruit and have thrived, and some are now considered weeds on disturbed sites across much of the United States. An example of such an introduced species is European mountain-ash.

What's In a Name?

Both common and scientific names are included for each plant. Scientific names are from the USDA PLANTS Database (www.plants.usda.gov), which were cross-referenced with our two major state-level botanical

European mountain-ash (*Sorbus aucuparia*)

authorities: the Burke Museum Herbarium at the University of Washington, and the Oregon Flora Project at Oregon State University. When necessary, E-Flora BC at the University of British Columbia was consulted for species with more northerly distributions, and CalFlora was consulted for species with more southerly distributions. As well, the old standard, *Flora of the Pacific Northwest* by Hitchcock and Cronquist, was used. Common names were drawn from all of these resources.

Common names are often confusing. Sometimes, the same common name can refer to a number of different, even unrelated, species. One common name can even refer to a plant that is edible and to a completely different and unrelated species that is poisonous! For this reason, the scientific name is included for each plant entry.

The two-part scientific name used by scientists to identify individual plants may look confusing, but it is a simple and universal system that is worth taking a few moments to learn about. Swedish botanist Carolus Linnaeus (1707–78) first suggested a system for grouping organisms into hierarchical categories, and it is still essentially the same today, almost 300 years after he first developed it! His system differed from other contemporary ones in that it used an organism's morphology (its form and structure) to categorize a species, with a particular emphasis on the reproductive parts, which we now know are the most ancient part of any plant. Another significant benefit of this hierarchical system is that it groups plants into families so that we can better understand and see how they are related to each other. For example, both oval-leaved blueberry (*Vaccinium ovalifolium*) and black huckleberry (*Vaccinium membranaceum*) are related cousins in the heath family (Ericaceae). In another example, Linnaeus' system shows us that roses are botanically related to apples—both are in the rose family (Rosaceae). Since the names of organisms in Linnaeus' system follow a standard format and are typically in Latin or Greek, they are the same in every language around the world, making this a truly universal classification and naming protocol.

In Linnaeus' system, the scientific name of a species has two parts: (1) the genus; and (2) a species identifier (or specific epithet), which is often a descriptive word. Both parts of the scientific name are written in italics, and the genus name is always capitalized. The first part of the scientific name, the genus, groups species that have common characteristics together. The second part, the specific epithet, which is not capitalized, often describes a physical or other characteristic of the organism, honors a person or suggests something about

the geographic range of the species. For example, in the scientific name for Cascade bilberry, *Vaccinium deliciosum*, the specific epithet roughly translates as "absolutely fantastically delicious." This apt name describes one of the best-tasting members of the blueberry/bilberry/huckleberry genus.

It is important to note, however, that botanists do not always agree on how some plants fit into this system. As a result, scientific names can change over time, or there can sometimes be more than one accepted scientific name for a plant. While this is somewhat annoying and may seem redundant, the important thing to remember is that one scientific name will never refer to more than one plant. Thus, if you have identified a wild berry as edible and know its scientific name(s), you can confirm that it is indeed edible and not have to worry that this name may refer to another (possibly deadly poisonous!) plant.

Botanists also sometimes further split species into subsets known as subspecies or varieties. For example, peaches and nectarines are two slightly different varieties of the peach tree,

Black huckleberry (*Vaccinium membranaceum*)

Prickly currant (*Ribes lacustre*)

19

Prunus persica. If you purchase a Harken peach tree at your local plant nursery, the tag should read "*Prunus persica*, variety Harken."

Giving Back to the Plants

While many of our native wild berries grow in profusion, others are threatened by habitat destruction, overharvesting or climate change. In some areas, harvesting is prohibited. Please do not dig up plants from the wild. Most berry species propagate easily from seed or cuttings, and you can also purchase healthy and responsibly produced plants from reputable nurseries. When you harvest native berries in the wild, it's nice to say "thank you" to the plant by weeding back competing species around its base, spreading some of its seeds in similar habitat a short distance from the parent plant or appropriately pruning the plant if you know the right technique. There is a long history of humans looking after the plants that support us; taking a few moments to continue this tradition and to teach it to our children is time well spent. By learning about our native berry species and harvesting them, we get to know and respect these plants and may even be moved to help protect and propagate them.

A Few Gathering Tips

1. Gather only species that are common and abundant, and never take all the fruit off one plant. Even then, a cautious personal quota will still deplete the plants if too many people gather them in one area. Remember, plants growing in harsh environments (e.g., northern areas, alpine, desert) might not have enough energy to produce flowers and fruits every year. Also, don't forget the local wildlife. The survival of many animals can depend on access to the fruits that you are harvesting.

2. Be sure to check whether or not berry picking is allowed, if a permit is needed and if there are legal limits to the amount of fruit you can pick in the area you are visiting.

3. Take only what you need, and damage the plant as little as possible. If you want to grow a plant in your garden, try propagating it from seed or a small cutting rather than transplanting it from the wild.

4. Don't take more than you will use. If you are gathering a plant for food, taste a sample. You may not like the taste of the berries, or the fruit at this site may not be as sweet and juicy as the ones you gathered last year.

5. Avoid polluted areas such as the sides of well-traveled roads. Heavy metals and other toxins can be absorbed and concentrated by plants.

6. Gather berries only when you are certain of their identity. Many irritating and poisonous plants grow wild in our region, and some of them resemble edible or medicinal species. If you are not positive that you have the right plant, don't use it. It is better to eat nothing at all than to be poisoned!

Recipes

Simple recipes for cooking, preserving or enjoying berries fresh off the plant are included throughout the book. Every berry gatherer or cook can produce delicious results to enjoy with friends and family in the heat of summer and later during the long winter months. The recipes call for specific berries, but you can experiment by substituting other fruit. For example, you could try replacing blueberries with serviceberries, cranberries or huckleberries.

Dried Fruit

It's hard to beat the flavor of home-dried wild berries. Enjoy these special treats out of the bag or add them to your favorite recipes in place of the usual commercial raisins, dried cranberries or blueberries.

Berries that dry well include huckleberries, strawberries, thimbleberries (which are a bit crunchy but have a fabulous flavor), blueberries, serviceberries, cranberries and currants. Berries that do not dry as well are seedier fruit such as blackberries or very juicy fruit such as salmonberries; it is better to mash these types of berries either alone or combined with other fruit and make them into fruit leather. Some fruit, such as elderberries, should be cooked before drying to neutralize the toxins present in the fresh fruit.

If some of the berries are much larger than others, cut them in half. All the berries on a tray should be roughly the same size to ensure even drying. Carefully pick through the fruit to remove insects and debris. Do not wash the berries—it will cause them to go mushy. Lightly grease a rimmed baking sheet and spread the berries on the sheet so that they do not touch each other. Place in a food dehydrator or dry in an oven at 140°F overnight, leaving the oven door ajar to allow moisture to escape. Cool and store the berries in an airtight container or resealable bags.

Frozen Wild Fruit the Easy Way

Freezing is the quickest and easiest way to preserve wild berries, allowing you to enjoy a wonderful snack any time of the year. Choose the best and ripest fruit and carefully remove all unwanted debris and insects. Some berries, such as elderberries, should be cooked first to neutralize any toxins. Give dusty berries a quick rinse, though the extra water and handling may bruise the fruits and stick them together during freezing.

Most instructions tell you to freeze berries individually on rimmed baking sheets before packing them in resealable bags. Used milk cartons are another option. Open the carton (1- or 2-quart size) fully and wash it well in warm, soapy water. Allow it to air dry. Cartons with a plastic lid and spout do not work for freezing. Unless a fruit is particularly mushy (like a very ripe wild raspberry), simply pick through the fruit to clean it, then gently pour the berries into the carton being careful not to let them pack too hard or crush. Push the top of the carton back together the way it was before opening, then firmly push the top edge so that it folds over flat and indents slightly so that it stays shut. Presto! A sealed container that will never get freezer burn, is easy to label on the top with a marker pen and stacks beautifully in the deep freeze!

To get the frozen fruit out, gently squeeze the carton sides to separate the berries, making it easy to pour out the desired quantity before resealing the carton and returning it to the freezer. If the berries are more firmly attached, simply place the carton on the floor and gently stand on it, turning the sides a few times. As a last resort, peel the carton down to the desired level, cut off the exposed fruit chunk with a sharp knife, and put the remainder of the carton in a resealable bag before replacing it in the freezer.

Northern gooseberry (*Ribes oxyacanthoides*)

A Cautionary Note

If you cannot correctly identify a plant, you should not use it. Identification is more critical with some plants than with others. For example, most people recognize strawberries and raspberries, and all of the species in these two groups are edible, though not all are equally palatable. Plants belonging to the nightshade family (Solanaceae), however, may be more difficult to distinguish from each other and can range from highly edible to poisonous. Even the most experienced harvesters still take time to carefully identify unknown plants. It is important to be certain of a species' identification and any special treatment required before eating a wild berry. Serviceberries, for example, are best cooked to neutralize the poisonous cyanide compounds found in their seeds and many types of under-ripe berries can cause digestive

upset or even be poisonous. Some rare individuals have an allergic reaction to certain berry species.

It is also important to know which parts of the berry are edible. For example, although the fleshy "berry" (it is really an "aril") of the Pacific yew tree is considered edible, eating this fruit is not recommended because the small, hard seed contained inside is so

Pacific yew (*Taxus brevifolia*)

Common juniper (*Juniperus communis*)

deadly poisonous that ingesting even a few can cause death! As a general rule, most of our native berry species taste good and are edible. Those berries that have a bitter, astringent or unpalatable taste are telling us that they are toxic or poisonous and that we should not be eating them. These species tend to rely on birds, rather than humans, to eat the fruit and distribute the seeds. The exceptions to these guidelines are the many introduced ornamental plants in our gardens and municipal plantings, some of which have naturalized into the wild and have sweet-tasting fruit. It is not recommended that you sample these non-native fruits without a positive identification. Examples of common poisonous berries are English holly, privet and any ornamental yew species.

Finally, some people believe that it is okay to eat berries that they see birds and wildlife enjoying. That is simply not the case, so do not test this flawed bit of folklore! Likewise, the fact that a plant has edible fruit does not mean that the plant itself is edible.

Pay attention to where you are harvesting. Fruit growing along the edge of a busy highway or near an industrial area could be contaminated with heavy metals or other pollutants. Municipal plantings might look delicious, but they may have been sprayed with pesticides and you might not be welcome to harvest the fruit if it has ornamental value. Please also remember to harvest on public, not private, lands unless you have received permission from the property owner.

Many plants have developed very effective protective mechanisms. Thorns and stinging hairs discourage animals from touching, let alone eating, many plants. Bitter, often irritating and poisonous compounds in leaves and roots repel grazing animals. Many protective devices are dangerous to humans. The **Warning** boxes throughout the book include notes of potential hazards associated with the plant(s) described. Hazards can range from deadly poisons to spines with irritating compounds in them. These Warning boxes may also describe poisonous plants that could be confused with the species being discussed in the account.

The line between delicious and dangerous is not always clearly defined. Many of the plants that we eat every day contain toxins, and almost any food is toxic if you eat too much of it. Personal sensitivities can also be important. People with allergies may die from eating common foods (e.g., peanuts) that are harmless to most of the population. Most wild plants are not widely used today, so their effects on a broad spectrum of society remain unknown.

As with many aspects of life, the best approach is "moderation in all things." Sample wisely—when trying something for the first time, take only a small amount to see how you like it and how your body reacts. Never feed a berry to other people that you haven't tried yourself several times.

No Two Plants Are the Same

Wild plants are highly variable. No two individuals of a species are identical, and many characteristics can vary. Some of the more easily observed characteristics include the color, shape and size of the stems, leaves, flowers and fruits. Other less obvious features, such as sweetness, toughness, juiciness and concentrations of toxins or other chemical compounds, also vary from one plant to the next.

Many factors control plant characteristics. Time is one of the most obvious.

Bitter cherry (*Prunus emarginata*)

All plants change as they grow and age. Usually, young leaves are the most tender, and mature fruits are the largest and sweetest. Underground structures also change throughout the year.

Habitat also has a strong influence on plant growth. The leaves of plants from moist, shady sites are often larger, sweeter and more tender than those of plants on dry, sunny hillsides. Berries may be plump and juicy one year, when shrubs have had plenty of moisture, but can become dry and wizened during a drought. Without the proper nutrients and environmental conditions, plants cannot grow and mature.

Finally, the genetic makeup of a species determines how the plant develops and how it responds to its environment. Wild plant populations tend to be much more variable than domestic crops, partly because of their wide range of habitats, but also because of their greater genetic variability.

Humans have been planting and harvesting plants for millennia, repeatedly selecting and breeding plants with the most desirable characteristics. This process has produced many highly productive cultivars—trees with larger, sweeter fruits, potatoes with bigger tubers and sunflowers with larger, oilier seeds. These crop species are more productive, and they also produce a specific product each time they are planted. Wild plants are much less reliable.

Wild species have developed from a broader range of ancestors growing in many different environments, so their genetic makeup is much more variable than that of domestic cultivars. One population may produce sweet, juicy berries, whereas the berries of another population may be small and tart; one plant may have low concentrations of a toxin that is plentiful in its neighbor. This variability makes wild plants much more resilient to

Salmonberry (*Rubus spectabilis*)

Red-osier dogwood (*Cornus sericea*)

change. Although their lack of stability may seem to reduce their value as crop species, it is one of their most valuable features. Domestic crops often have few defenses and must be protected from competition and predation. As fungi, weeds and insects continue to develop immunities to pesticides, we repeatedly return to wild plants for new repellents and, more recently, for pest-resistant genes for our crop plants.

Disclaimer

This book summarizes interesting, publicly available information about many plants in Washington and Oregon. It is not intended as a "how-to" guide for living off the land. Rather, it is a guide for people wanting to discover the astonishing biodiversity of our useful plants and to connect to our cultural traditions, especially those of Native Americans. Only some of the most widely used species in our region, and only some of their uses, are described and discussed. Self-medication with herbal medicines is not recommended. The use of plant medicines and consumption of wild foods should only be considered under guidance from an experienced healer, elder or herbalist. As a field guide, the information presented here is limited, and further study of species of interest should be made using other botanical literature. No plant or plant extract should be consumed unless you are absolutely certain of its identity and toxicity and of your personal potential for allergic reactions. The authors and publisher are not responsible for the actions of the reader.

THE BERRIES

Pacific Crab Apple *Malus fusca*

Also called: western crab apple, Oregon crab apple • *Pyrus fusca*

Pacific crab apple (*M. fusca*)

This is western North America's only native species of apple. The fruits of Pacific crab apple were an essential food item for Native Americans in the Pacific Northwest and are still highly valued today. Indeed, these trees were widely managed and carefully guarded resources that were often regarded as private property. Large quantities of crab apples were harvested in the past, typically from late summer into autumn, often after the first frost had softened the fruit.

Another method of harvest was to pick the crab apples in whole bunches when they were still hard and leave them to soften in baskets. They were either eaten fresh with fish or sea mammal oil or stored for winter. Because of their high acidity, crab apples keep extremely well without processing, becoming sweeter and softer over time. Traditionally, they were placed, raw or cooked, in bentwood cedar boxes or large watertight baskets lined with skunk cabbage leaves, then covered with water and a layer of animal grease.

Crab apples were sometimes an important part of ceremonial activities such as potlatches or large feasts. Historically, containers of Pacific crab apples were a common trade item and were also used as gifts at special events such as weddings. Pacific crab apples were also considered a fattening medicine and blood purifier. After a long day of hunting, the fruit was eaten to "kill poison in muscles."

Crab apples can be enjoyed canned, whole or made into juice, jelly, sauce or butter. The stems of whole crab apples can be more easily removed by first blanching the fruit. Add a tablespoon of sugar to each quart of apples, and let the jars "mature" for at least three months before opening them. The unsweetened juice makes an excellent substitute for lemon juice in

29

meringues and gives fermented ciders a lemonade-like flavor. Pacific crab apples are rich in pectin, so they can be added to low-pectin fruits when making jams and jellies.

EDIBILITY: highly edible, very sour

FRUIT: Egg-shaped crab apples, $3/8$–$5/8$ in across, green ripening to yellow, orange or purplish red, turning tan after a frost. Very tart and sour-tasting, but developing a sweetness and depth of flavor after a frost or storage that renders them quite tasty.

WARNING: *The bark and seeds of this tree contain cyanide compounds and should only be consumed under the guidance of a trained professional and with extreme caution.*

SEASON: Flowers late April through mid-May. Fruit ripens August and September, often staying on the tree well into winter if not eaten by wildlife.

DESCRIPTION: Deciduous small tree or tall shrub, 6–35 ft tall, scraggly in growth habit, with sharp spur-shoots. Bark rough, brown or grayish, older bark deeply fissured. Leaves alternate, 2–4 in long, elliptic to lance-shaped, toothed, 1–3 irregular lobes, pointed at tip, dark green to yellow-green above, paler and slightly hairy below, turning yellow and orange in fall. Flowers fragrant, white to pinkish, 5 showy petals, in flat-topped clusters. Found in estuary fringes, moist woods, wetlands and on streambanks and upper beaches along coastal areas, often growing in dense thickets.

31

Madrona   *Arbutus menziesii*

Also called: Pacific madrone, madrone, arbutus

Madrona (*A. menziesii*)

Native Americans in California sometimes ate madrona berries, but there is little record of its use in our area. Because the berries have a high tannin content, they are particularly astringent, especially if not fully ripe. To be stored over winter, they were first boiled or steamed, and then dried. They were soaked in warm water before being eaten. The berries can be crushed and made into a sweet cider or preserved as a jelly. A cider made from the berries was used to stimulate the appetite. Legend has it that the Saanich of southern Vancouver Island tied their canoes to madrona trees following the Great Flood; to this day, some Saanich people will not burn madrona wood because of the service it provided. Traditionally, the leaves and scarlet berries were used to make necklaces and decorations. Strung on thread, the berries make a natural Christmas garland that lasts well from year to year if stored properly.

EDIBILITY: edible

FRUIT: Orange-red berries with a rough, glandular surface, up to ⅜ in wide, containing several seeds, growing in upright to drooping clusters. Taste described as bland, mealy, astringent, bitter.

SEASON: Flowers April to May. Fruit ripens September to November.

DESCRIPTION: Small to medium, broadleaf, evergreen tree, to 100 ft tall (usually much shorter), with a wide, tropical-looking crown. Bark thin, smooth, reddish brown, peeling in papery flakes and strips, with newly exposed surfaces very soft to the touch (like a chamois cloth), yellowish green, soon reddening, thickening on old trunks and breaking into many small, dark brown flakes. Leaves alternate, simple, thick, leathery, oval to elliptic, 3–6 in long and 2–3 in wide. Flowers greenish white to white (sometimes pinkish), ¼ in long, with a sweet, honey-like fragrance, in drooping, branched clusters at the ends of branchlets. Grows in well-drained soils in dry, open forests and on exposed, rocky bluffs near sea level along the Pacific coast and Puget Sound. Southern British Columbia is the most northerly extent of its range; it is rarely found more than 5 mi inland or at elevations above 1000 ft.

WILD GARDENING: *Madrona is an extremely decorative tree that looks as if it belongs in the tropics rather than in coastal Washington and Oregon. Its berries are a cheerful, bright red-orange color, and with its glossy, evergreen leaves, it is a good choice for the ornamental or wildlife garden in all seasons.*

Junipers *Juniperus* spp.

Common juniper (*J. communis*)

Some tribes cooked ripe juniper berries into a mush and dried them in cakes for winter use. The berries were also dried whole and ground into a meal that was used to make mush and cakes. In times of famine, small pieces of the bitter bark or a few berries could be chewed to suppress hunger. Dried, roasted juniper berries have been ground and used as a coffee substitute, and teas were occasionally made from the stems, leaves and/or berries, but these concoctions were usually used as medicines rather than beverages. Juniper berries are well known for their use as a flavoring for gin, beer and other alcoholic drinks. A Tricky Mary can be made by soaking juniper berries in tomato juice for a few days, and then following the usual recipe for a Bloody Mary but omitting the gin. The taste is identical, and the drink is non-alcoholic.

Juniper berries can be quite sweet by the end of their second summer on the plant or the following spring, but they have a rather strong, "pitchy" flavor that some people find distasteful. They can be used to flavor meat dishes (especially venison and other wild game, veal and lamb), soups and stews, either whole, crushed or ground and used like pepper. Rocky mountain juniper sprigs were also sometimes placed among dried salmon or other stored foods to protect the food against insects and flies.

Juniper berry tea has been used to aid digestion, stimulate appetite, relieve colic and water retention, treat diarrhea and heart, lung and kidney problems, prevent pregnancy, stop bleeding, reduce swelling and inflammation and calm hyperactivity. The berries were chewed to relieve cold symptoms and settle upset stomachs. Oil of juniper (made from the berries) was mixed with fat to make a salve that would protect wounds from irritation by flies. Juniper berries are reported to stimulate urination by irritating the kidneys, but give the urine a violet-like fragrance. They are also said to stimulate sweating, mucus secretion, production of hydrochloric acid in the stomach and contractions in the uterus and intestines. Some studies have shown that juniper berries lower blood sugar caused by adrenaline hypergly-cemia, suggesting that they may be useful in the treatment of insulin-dependent diabetes. Juniper berries also have antiseptic qualities, and stud-ies by the National Cancer Institute have shown that some junipers contain antibiotic compounds that are active against tumors. Strong juniper tea has been used to sterilize needles and bandages, and during the Black Death in 14th-century Europe, doctors held

Common juniper (*J. communis*)

Common juniper (*J. communis*)

a few berries in the mouth, as they believed that this would prevent them from being infected by patients. During cholera epidemics in North America, some people drank and bathed in juniper tea to avoid infection. Juniper tea has been given to women in labor to speed delivery, and after the birth, it was used as a cleansing and healing agent.

Juniper berries were sometimes dried on strings, smoked over a greasy fire and polished to make shiny, black beads for necklaces. Some tribes also scattered berries to be used for necklaces on anthills. The ants would eat out the sweet centre, leaving a convenient hole for stringing. Smoke from the berries or branches of junipers has been used in religious ceremonies or to bring good luck (especially for hunters) or protection from disease, evil spirits, witches, thunder, lightning and so on. The berries make a pleasant, aromatic addition to potpourris, and vapors

Rocky Mountain juniper (*J. scopulorum*)

from boiling juniper berries in water were used to purify and deodorize homes affected by sickness or death.

These plants are decorative, particularly in the winter months, and make a hardy and drought-tolerant addition to an ornamental garden. Junipers can be very long-lived, with some recorded specimens as old as 1500 years.

EDIBILITY: edible, but with caution

FRUIT: Female plants bear small, fleshy cones ("berries"), 1/8–1/4 in wide, green maturing to bluish purple or bluish green.

SEASON: Berries form from May to June on female plants only, maturing the following year; they are ready to harvest by late summer and remain on the plant throughout winter.

DESCRIPTION: Coniferous, evergreen shrubs or small trees, to 65 ft tall, with some species creeping low on the ground. Leaves scale-like, opposite,

Common juniper (*J. communis*)

Seaside juniper (*J. maritima*)

Common juniper (*J. communis*)

Common juniper (*J. communis*)

dark green to yellowish, in rows. Male plants produce yellow pollen on cones ⅛ in long. Grows in open, dry, rocky areas and on grasslands.

Common juniper (*J. communis*) grows to 3 ft tall but is typically shorter. Growth habit is branching, prostrate, trailing, forming mats 3–10 ft wide. Leaves needle-like, dark green above, whitish below, prickly,

Rocky Mountain juniper (*J. scopulorum*)

½ in long, in whorls of 3. Bark reddish brown, scaly, thin and shredding. Grows on dry, open sites, along forest edges and gravelly ridges, and on muskeg, from lowland bogs to plains and subalpine zones. Found scattered throughout the Cascade, Klamath, Blue and Olympic mountain ranges. Also called: ground juniper, dwarf juniper.

Rocky Mountain juniper (*J. scopulorum*) is a less common species and grows to 50 ft tall. Leaves opposite, ¼ in long, in 4 vertical rows, young leaves often needle-like, mature leaves tiny and scale-like. Grows on dry, rocky ridges, open foothills, grasslands and bluffs in eastern Washington and northeastern Oregon.

WARNING: *Some reports consider juniper berries to be poisonous, and the leaves and oil of all junipers are toxic. Although the addition of a few berries to flavor a dish is likely safe, eating these berries regularly or in quantity is not advised. Large and/or frequent doses of juniper can result in convulsions, kidney failure and an irritated digestive tract. Pregnant women and people with kidney problems should never take any part of a juniper internally. Juniper oil is strong and can cause blistering.*

Western juniper (*J. occidentalis*)

Seaside juniper (*J. maritima*) Similar to Rocky Mountain juniper but with a range limited to Puget Sound, almost always growing directly adjacent to the coast on granite or sand. Seed cones mature in 14–16 months instead of the 2 years that it takes Rocky Mountain juniper cones to mature.

Western juniper (*J. occidentalis*) is a short-trunked, round-topped tree that commonly grows 15–20 ft tall. Leaves in groups of 3, in 6 vertical rows circling the round stems. Generally found at middle elevations in southeastern Washington and eastern Oregon on rocky or occasionally sandy slopes that are too dry for ponderosa pine (*Pinus ponderosa*).

Rocky Mountain juniper (*J. scopulorum*)

Hawthorns *Crataegus* spp.

Fireberry hawthorn (*C. chrysocarpa*)

The fruits, or haws, of all *Crataegus* species are edible, but the taste varies greatly depending on the species, time of year and growing conditions. Raw haws are rather seedy

English hawthorn (*C. monogyna*)

with a mealy texture and a flavor ranging from sweet to insipid to bitter. Frosts are known to increase the sweetness of the fruit. Historically, haws were eaten fresh from the tree or dried for winter use. The cooked, mashed pulp (with the seeds removed) was mixed with meat and fat to make pemmican, or dried and stored in cakes as a berry-bread, which could be added to soup or eaten with deer fat or marrow. Haws are rich in pectin, and if boiled with sugar, they can be a useful aid in getting jams and jellies to set without a commercial pectin product. They can also be steeped to make a pleasing tea or cold drink. English hawthorn fruits are commonly called

Black hawthorn (*C. douglasii*)

Black hawthorn (*C. douglasii*)

"bread and butter berries" in the UK, likely because of their starchy and somewhat creamy texture.

Hawthorn flowers and fruits are famous in herbal medicine as heart tonics, though not all species are equally effective. Studies have supported the use of hawthorn extracts as a treatment for high blood pressure associated with a weak heart, angina pectoris (recurrent pain in the chest and left arm owing to a sudden lack of blood in the heart muscle) and arteriosclerosis (loss of elasticity and thickening of the artery walls). Hawthorn is believed to slow the heart rate and reduce blood pressure by dilating the large arteries that supply blood to the heart and by acting as a mild heart stimulant. However, hawthorn has a gradual, mild action and must be taken for extended periods to produce noticeable results. Hawthorn tea has also been used to treat kidney disease and nervous conditions such as insomnia. Dark-colored haws are especially high in flavonoids and can be steeped in hot water to make teas for strengthening connective tissues damaged by inflammation. Haws were sometimes eaten in moderate amounts to relieve diarrhea (some indigenous peoples considered them very constipating).

The genus name *Crataegus* is derived from the Greek *kratos*, which means "strength" and refers to the hardness and durability of the wood. The common name "hawthorn" is derived from the Old English word for a hedge, or "haw"; the species was historically planted and worked into hedgerows, where its spiky thorns, branching nature and durable wood made a formidable and lasting barrier.

EDIBILITY: edible, with poor to mediocre flavor

FRUIT: Small, pulpy, red to purplish pomes (tiny apples) containing 1–5 nutlets and hanging in bunches.

English hawthorn (*C. monogyna*)

SEASON: Flowers May to June. Fruit ripens late August to September.

DESCRIPTION: Deciduous shrubs or small trees 20–45 ft tall, with strong, straight thorns growing directly from younger branches. Leaves alternate, generally oval with a wedge-shaped base. Flowers whitish, 5-petaled, sometimes unpleasant-smelling, forming showy, flat-topped clusters.

Black hawthorn (*C. douglasii*) grows to 35 ft tall, with thorns ½–3 in long. Leaves toothed to shallowly lobed. Flowers white with 10 stamens. Fruits ½ inch long, purplish black or red, ripening in August. Grows along forest edges, in thickets and along stream-sides and roadsides in lowland to montane zones throughout our area. Plants with thorns 2–3 in long and red fruit found exclusively east of the Cascades were formerly called Columbia hawthorn (*C. columbiana* var. *columbiana*) but are now lumped with black hawthorn by taxonomists. Also called: thorn apple.

English hawthorn (*C. monogyna*) grows 15–45 ft tall, with thorns ½–1 in long on younger stems. Bark dull brown, sometimes with orange-shaded cracks. Leaves dark on top, paler underneath, 1–2 in long, obovate, deeply lobed sometimes to the midrib. Fruits dark red, ⅜ in long, with a single, hard seed. Introduced to Washington and western Oregon but native to Europe, northwestern Africa and western Asia. Also called: common hawthorn, oneseed hawthorn, May tree.

Fireberry hawthorn (*C. chrysocarpa*) grows to 20 ft tall, with thorns 1–3 in long and dark red, egg-shaped haws. Haws ripen in July and are perhaps the best-tasting native hawthorn fruits in our area. The haws can be strained to remove the seeds to make pie filling or dried to make fruit leather. Grows in open prairies and meadows, and along streambanks and forest edges in steppe and montane zones northeastern

Fireberry hawthorn (*C. chrysocarpa*)

Oregon. Two named varieties exist: red hawthorn (var. *chrysocarpa*) and Piper's hawthorn (var. *piperi*).

Suksdorf's hawthorn (*C. suksdorfii*) grows 3–40 ft high, with thorns ¼–½ in long. Bark scaly, rough, pale gray-brown on younger branches, gray on older wood. Leaves 1–3 in long, oblong to elliptic, alternate, simple, pinnate, margins double-toothed. Haws black, shiny, smooth. Differentiated from black hawthorn by having significantly shorter thorns, leaves often fewer-lobed and flowers with 20 stamens (very occasionally 15). Found in meadows, on dry hillsides and in riparian areas in western and northeastern Oregon. Tends to grow at higher elevations than black hawthorn. Also called: Klamath hawthorn
• *C. douglasii* var. *suksdorfii*.

Black hawthorn (*C. douglasii*)

Black hawthorn (*C. douglasii*)

Piper's hawthorn (*C. chrysocarpa* var. *piperi*)

Suksdorf's hawthorn (*C. suksdorfii*)

Mountain-ashes *Sorbus* spp.

Sitka mountain-ash (*S. sitchensis*)

The bitter-tasting fruits of these trees are high in vitamin C and can be eaten raw, cooked or dried. Just outside our area, in southern British Columbia, the Halkome'lem, Lillooet, Nlaka'pamux and Okanagon peoples are known to have consumed Sitka mountain-ash fruit, and it was possibly eaten by the Okanagon-Coleville in north-central Washington as well. After picking, these berries were sometimes stored fresh underground for later use. They were also added to other more popular berries or used to marinate meat such as marmot or to flavor salmon head soup. The berries ripen to various shades of red in late summer and early fall, and the bitter fruit reportedly mellows with repeated frosts.

Mountain-ash fruit has been used to make jams, jellies, pies, ale and bittersweet wine, and it is also enjoyed cooked and sweetened. In northern Europe, the berries, which can be quite mealy, were historically dried and ground into flour, which was fermented and used to make a strong liquor. A tea made from the berries is astringent and has been used as a gargle for relieving sore throats and tonsillitis.

Western mountain-ash (*S. scopulina*)

European mountain-ash fruit has been used medicinally to make teas for treating indigestion, hemorrhoids, diarrhea and problems with the urinary tract, gallbladder and heart. Some indigenous peoples rubbed the berries into their scalps to kill lice and treat dandruff. European mountain-ash is a popular ornamental tree, and native mountain-ashes make attractive garden shrubs, easily propagated from seed sown in fall. The scarlet fruits can persist throughout winter, and the bright clusters attract many birds.

EDIBILITY: edible, but not great

FRUIT: Berry-like pomes, about ⅓ in long, hanging in clusters.

SEASON: Blooms June to July. Fruit ripens August to September.

DESCRIPTION: Clumped, deciduous shrubs or trees growing to 35 ft tall. Bark smooth, brownish, with numerous lenticels (raised ridges that are actually

European mountain-ash (*S. aucuparia*)

breathing pores) on young bark, turning gray and rough with age. Leaves alternate on the stem, compound,

California mountain-ash (*S. californica*)

45

pinnately divided into 11–17 leaflets. Leaflets sharply toothed, narrow, darker above, paler below. Flowers white, about ⅜ in across, 5-petaled, smelly, in flat-topped clusters 4–6 inches wide. Grows in sun-dappled woods, on rocky ridges and along forest edges, preferring moist areas and partial to full sun.

California mountain-ash (*S. californica*) is a shrub 2–9 ft tall, formerly considered to be a subspecies of Sitka mountain-ash. Bark smooth, reddish. Leaves have 7–9 finely toothed leaflets. Pomes scarlet red, round, ⅓ in wide, in flat-topped clusters. In our region, the range is limited to Klamath County in Oregon on sites above 5000 ft, but it is

European mountain-ash (*S. aucuparia*)

European mountain-ash (*S. aucuparia*)

Western mountain-ash (*S. scopulina*)

more widespread in northern California and the Sierra Nevada

European mountain-ash (*S. aucuparia*) is a widely planted ornamental tree, to 50 ft tall, with white-hairy buds, leaf stems and leaves (at least on underside), and orange to red fruits. This Eurasian species is widely cultivated and just as widely escaped. Found in western and southern Washington and northwestern Oregon. Also called: rowan tree.

Western mountain-ash (*S. scopulina*)

Sitka mountain-ash (*S. sitchensis*) is a tall shrub, to 12 ft, with rusty-hairy (but not sticky) twigs and buds. Leaves with 7–11 dull, bluish green, round-tipped leaflets without teeth near the base. Fruit crimson to purplish. Grows in foothill to subalpine zones in western and northern Washington and in most counties in Oregon.

Western mountain-ash (*S. scopulina*) is a tall shrub, to 15 ft, with sticky twigs and buds. Leaves have 9–13 shiny, green, pointed leaflets, with teeth almost to the base. Fruit orange. Grows in moist to wet, open forests and glades, from streambanks to higher elevations. Present in all but the driest counties in Washington and Oregon. Western mountain-ash has the best-tasting fruit of all our native mountain-ash species. Also called: Greene's mountain-ash.

ld Roses   *Rosa* spp.

Swamp rose (*R. pisocarpa*)

Most parts of rose shrubs are edible, and the fruits, called "hips," which remain on the branches throughout winter, are available when most other species have finished for the season. The hips can be eaten fresh or dried and are most commonly used to make tea, jam, jelly, syrup and wine. Usually only the fleshy outer layer is eaten (see Warning, p. 51). Because rose hips are so seedy, some indigenous peoples considered them to be a famine food rather than regular fare.

Rose hips are rich in vitamins A, B, E and K and are one of our best native sources of vitamin C. Three hips can contain as much as a whole orange! During World War II, when oranges could not be imported, British and Scandinavian people collected hundreds of tons of rose hips to make nutritious syrup. The vitamin C content of fresh hips varies greatly, but that of commercial "natural" rose hip products can fluctuate even more.

Rose petals have a delicate rose flavor with a hint of sweetness and may be eaten alone as a trail nibble, added to teas, jellies and wines or candied. Adding a few rose petals to a regular salad instantly turns it into a delicious gourmet conversation piece, and guests are often surprised at how delicate and sweetly delicious the petals taste. Do not add commercial rose petals to salads, however, as they are often sprayed with chemicals.

Rose petals have been taken to relieve colic, heartburn, headaches and mouth sores. They were also ground and mixed with grease to make a salve for mouth sores or mixed with wine to make a medicine for relieving earaches, toothaches and uterine cramps. Dried rose petals have a lovely fragrance and are a common ingredient in potpourri.

The tender young shoots of many roses can also be snapped off, peeled and eaten fresh. They have a mild, sweet flavor. Rose sprigs were traditionally hung on cradleboards to keep ghosts away from babies and on the walls of haunted houses and placed in graves to prevent the dead from howling. During pit cooking, the leaves of Nootka rose were placed under and over food to add flavor and to prevent food close to the bottom of the pit from burning. Hunters made a wash from Nootka rose branches to mask their human scent.

Some native roses can hybridize with each other, resulting in offspring that have mixed traits.

EDIBILITY: edible raw, incredible when made into jelly

FRUIT: Scarlet to purplish, round to pear-shaped, berry-like hips, ½–1 in long, with a fleshy outer layer enclosing many stiff-hairy achenes (seeds).

SEASON: Blooms June to August. Hips ripen August to September.

DESCRIPTION: Deciduous shrubs and vines with stems that are often armed with sharp prickles. Leaves alternate, compound, pinnately divided into about 5–7 oblong, toothed leaflets, generally odd in number. Flowers light pink to deep rose, 5-petaled, fragrant, usually growing at branch tips. Found in a wide range of habitats including dry, rocky slopes, forest edges, woodlands

and clearings, roadsides and streamsides at middle to low elevations.

Baldhip rose (*R. gymnocarpa*) is a small shrub generally less than 4 ft tall (but can be up to 9 ft tall) with few to abundant soft prickles. Flowers dark

Nootka rose (*R. nutkana*)

Baldhip rose (*R. gymnocarpa*)

Dog rose (*R. canina*)

49

pink, small, in clusters roughly 1 in wide. Hips ¼–⅓ in wide. Sepals at the end of hips fall off as the fruits mature, hence the common name for this species. Grows throughout Washington and Oregon. Also called: dwarf rose.

California rose (*R. californica*) is a shrub 3–10 ft tall with few to many thick-based, flattened prickles that are generally curved. Leaves with leaflets up to 1 in long. Flowers pink. Hips spherical to pear-shaped, roughly ⅓–½ in wide. Found in both southwestern and northwestern Oregon. Similar species: Smaller plants with shorter leaflets may be prairie rose. California rose is considered by some botanists to be a variety of prairie rose.

Cascade rose (*R. yainacensis*) is a low, spreading bramble, densely armed with long, straight prickles. Leaves usually with 7 leaflets, green above, pale and fuzzy below. Found in southern Oregon east of the Cascades.

Nootka rose (*R. nutkana*)

California rose (*R. californica*)

Ground rose (*R. spithamea*)

Swamp rose (*R. pisocarpa*)

50

Dog rose (*R. canina*) is an introduced species with stout, recurved prickles. Leaves have a smooth lower surface. Flowers white-pink, petals 1 in long, sepals long, often with slender lateral lobes. Hips ½–1 in wide with reflexed sepals that fall off. Common along roadsides in Puget Sound and throughout Oregon.

Glandular rose (*R. myriadenia*) is a low-branching briar with curved prickles at leaf joints. Leaves have 5 oval leaflets with sawtoothed margins, wooly undersides and glandular veins and margins. Flowers in clusters of 1–3. Found in Jackson County, Oregon.

Ground rose (*R. spithamea*) is a low, brambling plant generally less than 1 ft tall. Stems armed with straight prickles at leaf joints and often covered with smaller bristles. Hips conspicuously covered in glandular hairs. Grows in open forests in southwestern Oregon.

Multiflora rose (*R. multiflora*) forms massive briars up to 33 ft wide and

WARNING: *The dry inner "seeds" (achenes) of the hips are not palatable, and their fiberglass-like hairs can irritate the digestive tract and cause "itchy bum" if ingested. As kids, we used to make a great old-fashioned itching powder by slicing a ripe hip in half and scraping out the seeds with these attached hairs. Spread this material to dry, then swirl it in a bowl, and the seeds will drop to the bottom. Skim off the fine, dry hairs, and this is your itching powder, guaranteed to work. Although all members of the rose family have cyanide-like compounds in their seeds, drying or cooking destroys these compounds.*

Baldhip rose (*R. gymnocarpa*)

Prairie rose (*R. woodsii*)

Cultivated sweetbriar rose (*R. micrantha*)

Sweetbriar rose (*R. eglanteria*)

10 ft tall. This ornamental rose is becoming problematic in some natural areas. Flowers ½–¾ in wide, in clusters of 25–100 or more. Hips ¼ in across. Found in disturbed areas and riparian zones.

Nootka rose (*R. nutkana*) is a small shrub to 6 ft tall, with 2 well-developed thorns at leaf joints and generally no prickles except occasionally on new wood. Flowers light pink, large (2–3 in wide), mostly single. Hips ½–1 in long. Grows in moist, open areas, including shorelines, forest edges, streambanks and roadsides in most of the forested counties of Washington and Oregon.

Prairie rose (*R. woodsii*) is a shrub 2–4 ft tall, with well-developed, curved thorns and no prickles on upper stems (small prickles can be abundant on older growth closer to the ground). Leaves with coarsely toothed leaflets, usually less than ¾ in long. Flowers ½–¾ in wide, usually in small clusters. Hips spherical, ¼–½ inch wide. Grows in thickets, on prairies and along riverbanks east of the Cascades in Washington and Oregon. Also called: Woods' rose. Similar species: California rose is nearly identical to prairie

rose but can grow to 10 ft tall and has larger leaflets.

Rugosa rose (*R. rugosa*) is a robust ornamental commonly planted in hedgerows and urban landscaping. Plants form dense thickets 3–6 ft tall, with new shoots suckering from the roots. Branches covered with a dense layer of prickles ⅛–⅜ in long. Leaves 3–6 in long, with 5–9 large, egg-shaped leaflets. Flowers usually dark pink (sometimes white), 2½–3½ in across. Hips larger than any other species covered here, reaching just over 1 in long and persisting through winter.

Multiflora rose (*R. multiflora*)

Rosehip Jelly

Makes 8 x 1 cup jars

2 lbs whole rosehips · 2 lbs apples · 5 cups water · juice of 1 lemon
6 to 8 cloves · small cinnamon stick · white sugar

Carefully wash rosehips and apples. *While any ripe rosehips will work, in my experience, those of the swamp rose have the most superior flavor. Slightly unripe apples work best for this recipe as they have a higher pectin content than ripe fruit does.* Core apples and chop roughly. Place the apples and rosehips in separate cooking pans with 2½ cups of water in each pan. Add lemon juice, cloves and cinnamon to the pan containing the rosehips. Bring both pans gently to the boil, then reduce heat and simmer until the fruit is soft and pulpy. Place the contents of both pans together in a jellybag and allow the juice to strain through overnight into a clean bowl. *If you want a perfectly clear jelly, do not press or squeeze the bag.*

In the morning, measure the strained liquid and allow for 2 cups of sugar to every 2½ cups of juice. Place the juice and sugar in a thick-bottomed cooking pan. *A thick-bottomed pan is important, because a thin-bottomed pan will get too hot and scald the jelly.* Bring to the boil, stirring and being careful to scrape the bottom of the pan, until the sugar is dissolved. Boil until setting point is reached (this is when you take some of the liquid on a wide-lipped spoon, blow on it to cool, then start to pour it off the side of the spoon and it gels together). Meanwhile, prepare 8 x 1 cup jars and lids (wash and sterilize jars and lids, and fill jars with boiling water; drain just before use).

Pour the hot jelly into the clean, hot, sterilized jars. Seal the jars and place out of the sun to cool.

Swamp rose (*R. pisocarpa*) grows 1½–6 ft tall. Leaflets sharp-pointed, with paired prickles at leaf joints (similar to Nootka rose). Flowers small, less than 2 in across, in clusters. Hips less than ½ in wide with persistent, bristly haired sepals. Flowers and fruit mature 2–4 weeks after those of Nootka rose. Inhabits western Washington and most of Oregon, usually in or very near wetlands. Also called: clustered wild rose, cluster rose.

Sweetbriar rose (*R. eglanteria*) is a lanky shrub introduced from Europe, 4–8 ft tall, with flat, recurved prickles. Leaves have 5–7 sawtooth-margined leaflets with fuzzy, aromatic undersides. Flowers white-pink. Hips ⅜ in wide, ⅝ in long, smooth with a few prickles and bristly haired sepals that fall off. Found in western Washington and western Oregon. Similar species: *R. micrantha* is another cultivated sweetbriar that can be found on old home sites. It has flowers with smooth styles.

Rugosa rose (*R. rugosa*)

Red Cherries   *Prunus* spp.

Bitter cherry (*P. emarginata*)

Sour cherry (*P. cerasus*)

Many of these cherries may be eaten raw as a tart nibble, but the cooked or dried fruit is much sweeter, and additional sugar further improves the flavor. The fruit can be cooked in pies, muffins, pancakes and other baking, or strained and made into jelly, syrup, juice, sauce or wine. Cherries seldom contain enough natural pectin to make a firm jelly, so pectin must be added (try hawthorns or Pacific crab apple for a natural source rather than store-bought preparations). Although wild cherries are small compared to domestic varieties, they can be collected in large quantities. Pitting such small fruits is a tedious job if you are trying to keep the fruit intact, especially because they are too tiny to use with a cherry-pitting tool. However, a fruit mill does a fine job of separating the pits from the pulp if you are making sauces, jam or fruit leather.

Bitter cherry fruit, as the common name suggests, is bitter-tasting and not very nice to eat without being sweetened, especially if not fully ripe. When in flower, the sweet cherry tree is a dramatic and sweet-scented pleasure to behold so is well worth considering as an addition to an ornamental garden.

Wild cherry trees are worth growing in an ornamental or habitat garden as the fruit is a favorite food for mammals such as chipmunks, rabbits, mice, deer, elk and moose, and birds such as robins and grouse.

EDIBILITY: varies by species, ranging from highly edible to very bitter

FRUIT: Fleshy drupes (cherries) ranging in color from red to blackish purple to black, with large stones (pits).

SEASON: Flowers April to June. Fruit ripens July to August.

DESCRIPTION: Deciduous shrubs or small trees 5–80 ft tall. Trunk and branches reddish brown, often shiny, with raised horizontal pores (lenticels)

prominent in stripes on the trunk and larger branches. Leaves smooth, finely toothed, sharp-tipped, 1–5 in long. Flowers white or pinkish, about $\frac{1}{2}$ in across, 5-petaled, solitary, in small groups or long racemes.

Bitter cherry (*P. emarginata*)

Sweet cherry (*P. avium*)

55

Bitter cherry (*P. emarginata*) grows to 50 ft tall. Bark reddish brown or gray. Young twigs very long and slender with short spur-branches on 2nd- and 3rd-year growth. Leaves finely rounded at tip, 1–4 in long, oblong to oval, stalked, 1–2 small glands at the base of the leaf blade, blunt-toothed with no prominent point (note leaf shape, fruit color and number of clustered fruits to differentiate this species from pin cherry). Flowers white to pinkish, 5–10 in flat-topped clusters 4–6 in across. Flowers bloom during leaf-out from late April through May (a month after those of sweet cherry). Fruit red to black cherries $\frac{3}{8}$–$\frac{1}{2}$ in long, ripening in August, very bitter. Grows in moist, sparsely wooded areas along stream-banks or in cleared fields, on hillsides and in open or disturbed areas throughout Washington and Oregon. Known to hybridize with sweet cherry, especially in Puget Sound.

Cherry laurel (*P. laurocerasus*) is a small tree 15–50 ft tall. Leaves evergreen, leathery, shiny, 5–10 in long, with finely toothed margins.

WARNING: *Cherry leaves, bark, wood and seeds (stones) contain hydrocyanic acid and therefore can cause cyanide poisoning. The flesh of the cherry is the only edible part. The stone should always be discarded, but cooking or drying destroys the toxins. Cherry leaves and twigs can be poisonous to browsing animals.*

Flowers in upright racemes of 30–40 flowers each. Fruit $\frac{1}{3}$–$\frac{2}{3}$ in wide, black, bland. Although the ripe fruit pulp is edible, it should not be eaten if any bitterness is detected because it may contain hydrocyanic acid (especially when unripe). Introduced from Eurasia as a hedge plant, occasionally escaping west of the Cascades. Also called: hedge laurel.

Mahaleb cherry (*P. mahaleb*) is a small tree usually less than 35 ft tall. Leaves broadly ovate with abruptly narrowing, sharp-pointed tips. Flowers grow from current year's new growth on a branched flower stalk. Fruits red, maturing to dark purple or black, $\frac{1}{3}$–$\frac{1}{2}$ in across,

Sand cherry (*P. pumila*)

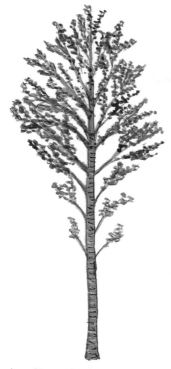

very bitter. Introduced from Eurasia, where it is used as a spice, Mahaleb cherry is uncommon in a few counties in eastern Washington and western and northeastern Oregon.

Sand cherry (*P. pumila*) is a small shrub rarely exceeding 6 ft tall. Cherries ½ in wide, ripening to dark purple in early summer. Forms dense thickets on dry soils. Known in our area only from Klamath County, Oregon.

Bitter cherry (*P. emarginata*)

Bitter cherry (*P. emarginata*)

Bitter cherry (*P. emarginata*)

Sweet cherry (*P. avium*)

Sour cherry (*P. cerasus*) is similar to sweet cherry but shorter (15–35 ft tall), with smaller leaves (2–3 in long) that are hairless on the underside. Introduced from Eurasia to a few counties in northwestern and southeastern Washington, rare in Oregon.

Sweet cherry (*P. avium*) is a nicely formed, straight tree 50–100 ft tall. Leaves 4–6 in long, downy on the underside, at least along the main vein, with 2 distinct, red glands on the leaf stalks (petioles). Flowers white, ¾ in across, stems (peduncles) 1–2 in long, several flowers arising from the tips of the previous year's growth on spur branches in a loose cluster. Flowers begin blooming before leaf-out in late

Mahaleb cherry (*P. mahaleb*)

Sand cherry (*P. pumila*)

March or early April and last for about a month. Cherries ½–1 in wide, ripening from late June to early July, ranging in taste from sweet to slightly bitter. Introduced from Eurasia, sweet cherry is found in all but the driest counties in Washington and west of the Cascades in Oregon. Hybridizes with bitter cherry where both species occur.

Sweet cherry (*P. avium*)

Cherry laurel (*P. laurocerasus*)

Sour cherry (*P. cerasus*)

Chokecherry *Prunus virginiana*

Also called: wild cherry

Chokecherry (*P. virginiana*)

Chokecherries were among the most important and widely used berries by Native Americans in North America. In our area, these fruits were highly regarded, especially among Native Americans east of the Cascades. They were collected after a frost (which makes them much sweeter) and then dried or cooked, often as an addition to pemmican or stews. Large quantities were gathered, pulverized with rocks, formed into patties about 6 in in diameter and 1 in thick and dried for winter use. Chokecherries were most commonly dried with the pits intact (a process

people, the ripening chokecherry fruits signaled that the Chinook salmon were coming up the river to spawn (in scientific circles, this is called a "phenological indicator," where the appearance or life stage of one organism signifies a corresponding stage in another organism). Dried chokecherries were an important trade item for some Native Americans.

EDIBILITY: highly edible when fully ripe, after a frost, dried or sweetened

that destroys the toxic hydrocyanic acid in the pits); they could also be stored for several months when picked as branches and kept in a cool, dry place. Today, chokecherries are used to make beautifully colored jelly, syrup, sauce and beer, as well as wine.

Raw chokecherries are sour and astringent, particularly if they are not fully ripe, and cause a puckering or choking sensation when they are eaten—hence the common name "chokecherry." One unimpressed early European traveler in 1634 is reported to have written that "chokecherries so furre the mouthe that the tongue will cleave the roofe, and the throate wax hoarse." After they have been cooked or dried, however, chokecherries are much sweeter and lose their characteristic astringency.

Dried, powdered cherry flesh was taken to improve appetite and relieve diarrhea and bloody discharge from the bowels. For the Okanagon-Colville

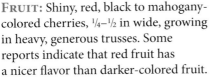

FRUIT: Shiny, red, black to mahogany-colored cherries, ¼–½ in wide, growing in heavy, generous trusses. Some reports indicate that red fruit has a nicer flavor than darker-colored fruit.

SEASON: Flowers May to June. Fruit ripens August to September.

DESCRIPTION: Deciduous shrub or most often small tree growing to 25 ft tall. Bark smooth, grayish, marked with small, horizontal slits (slightly raised pores called lenticels). Leaves alternate, 1–5 in long, broadly oval, finely sharp-toothed, with 2–3 prominent glands near the stalk tip. Flowers creamy white, ⅓–½ in across, 5-petaled, in hanging,

bottlebrush-like clusters 2–6 in long. Found in deciduous woods, open sites and along streams and forest edges.

WARNING: *As with other species of* Prunus *and* Pyrus, *all parts of the chokecherry except the flesh of the fruit contain cyanide-producing glycosides. There are reports of children dying after eating large amounts of fresh chokecherries without removing the stones. Cooking or drying the seeds, however, appears to destroy most of the toxins. Chokecherry leaves and twigs are poisonous to animals.*

Plums *Prunus* spp.

Cherry plum (*P. cerasifera*)

Plums, along with only a handful of other North American fruit plants, have been cultivated and play an important role in our modern food economy. Although none of our native species (American and Klamath plums) grow in abundance in our region, Native Americans enjoyed the fruit wherever it could be found, and it was pitted and dried for use throughout the year. Native Americans also used many parts of American plum medicinally. The Cherokee used the bark to make a cough syrup and to treat kidney and bladder ailments.

Many groups used an infusion or poultice made from the roots to treat mouth and skin sores.

EDIBILITY: edible, with raw fruit ranging from sweet to astringent and bitter (frost, removing the skin and cooking sweeten the fruit)

FRUIT: Typically 1 in wide or less, ranging in color from green to red to black. Filled with a single, large pit.

SEASON: Among the first shrubs to flower in spring. Fruit ripens mid- to late summer.

DESCRIPTION: Plums and cherries can be difficult to distinguish when not in fruit, but plums usually have larger, shorter-stalked flowers with fewer per cluster. All our plums are more or less shrubby in nature; most usually have thorns. Leaves alternate, with sawtoothed margins. Flowers white or pink, with 5 regular petals. In all members of this genus, the twigs release a pungent aroma when scratched with a thumbnail.

American plum (*P. americana*) is a large shrub reaching 15 ft tall. Bark dark purple-brown. Branches occasionally sharp-tipped. Leaves 2–4 in long, often hairy beneath, with stout, fuzzy petioles (leaf stalks). Commonly cultivated for its beautiful white flowers, used as grafting stock or planted in hedgerows. Flowers and fruit borne in clusters of 2–5 from spur branches. Plums up to 1 in wide, orange to purple-red skin, yellow flesh, ranging in flavor from sour to sweet. Possibly found in isolated patches in Whitman and Klickitat Counties in Washington and Wallowa and Baker Counties in Oregon; more typically found east of the Rockies. Also called: wild plum.

Blackthorn (*P. spinosa*) is a thorny shrub 3–15 ft tall. Young twigs often blackish, covered with downy hairs. Spur branches give rise to 1 to several single-stalked flowers before leafing out. Leaves 1–2 in long, dull green. Plums round, bluish black with a waxy, light blue bloom, ⅓–½ in wide, harvested after first frost, astringent flavor. Introduced from Eurasia to a few counties in southwestern and southeastern Washington and western Oregon.

Blackthorn plum (*P. spinosa*)

Cherry plum (*P. cerasifera*) is a large, occasionally spined shrub or small, scraggly tree 20–50 ft tall. Leaves 2–3 in long, green (or red in one variety), underside midrib hairy, petioles without glands. Flowers white, 1 in across, borne singly or in pairs in leaf axils or on very short (⅛ in long) spur branches. Plums 1 in wide, yellow, red or purple, ranging in flavor from sour to sweet. Introduced from Eurasia but has escaped cultivation in western and southeastern Washington and western and northeastern Oregon. Commonly used as rootstalk for other plums and as an ornamental, and is thought to be the ancestor of all European plum (*P. domestica*) varieties.

American plum (*P. americana*)

WARNING: *The leaves, bark, wood and seeds (stones) of all plums contain hydrocyanic acid and can cause cyanide poisoning. The flesh of the plum is the only edible part of the plant. The stone should always be discarded, but cooking or drying destroys the toxins. Plum leaves and twigs can be poisonous to browsing animals.*

Cherry plum (*P. cerasifera*)

Klamath plum (*P. subcordata*) is a small, spiny shrub to 10 ft tall. Bark grayish. Leaves 1–2 in long. Flowers white-pink, in clusters of 1–4 arising from branch tips. Plums dark red to purple, 1 in long, tart flavor. Found in non-coastal southern Oregon and rarely northward in the Willamette Valley. Also called: Oregon plum, Sierra plum.

Klamath plum (*P. subcordata*)

American plum (*P. americana*)

American plum (*P. americana*)

Cherry plum (*P. cerasifera*)

Indian-plum   *Oemleria cerasiformis*

Also called: bird plum, oso-berry, skunk bush • *Osmaronia cerasiformis, Nuttallia cerasiformis*

Indian-plum (*O. cerasiformis*)

The berries of Indian-plum were eaten fresh or dried by Native Americans in western Washington and Oregon. The fruit has only a thin layer of flesh covering the large, single seed, which makes it rather labor intensive to prepare or consume. Because the fruits are very bitter before they become fully ripe, some Native Americans referred to Indian-plum as "choke cherry." The fruit reportedly tastes best when changing from red to purple. It was eaten fresh, dried or cooked, typically at family meals or at large feasts, and was also sometimes covered with oil and stored in cedar boxes for winter eating.

Ground squirrels and other rodents, as well as birds, deer, foxes and coyotes eat this fruit. Indian-plum is one of our first native species to bloom in spring, and the flowers are an important early nectar source for bees and other insects.

The species name *cerasiformis* means "cherry-like." Another common name for Indian-plum is "oso-berry"—*oso* means "bear," and these animals are known to relish this fruit.

EDIBILITY: edible; the peculiar flavor makes this fruit more of a novelty food than a staple

FRUIT: Fleshy drupes resembling bunches of small plums, with a mild but distinctive cucumber flavor, about ⅓ in long, green then peach-colored when unripe, bluish black when ripe, with a large pit, borne on a red stem.

SEASON: Flowers April to May. Fruit ripens in June.

DESCRIPTION: Deciduous shrub or small tree, 5–20 ft tall. Bark smooth and gray, reddish to purplish on new twigs. Leaves alternate, 2–5 in long, lance-shaped to oblong, smelling like cucumber or watermelon rind when crushed, light green and smooth above, paler beneath. Flowers greenish white, ¼ in across, male and female flowers similar but borne on separate plants, generally appearing before leaves, in clusters hanging from leaf axils, strong-smelling (male flowers said to smell like cat urine; female flowers with cucumber or watermelon rind odor). Found at low elevations in dry to moist, open woods, along rivers and streambanks and in clearings west of the Cascades in Washington and Oregon.

Smooth Sumac *Rhus glabra*

Smooth sumac (*R. glabra*)

Smooth sumac's showy, red fruit clusters are beautiful to look at and can be made into a refreshing and pretty, pink or rose-colored drink that has a lemonade-like flavor. Crush the berries, then soak the mash in cold water before straining to remove the fine hairs from the fruit and other debris. The juice is best sweetened with sugar and served cold. Boiling the fruit in hot water releases tannins and produces a bitter-tasting liquid. The fruit has also been used to make jellies or lemon pies. Tangy, lemon-flavored sumac fruit (the flavor really comes from the hairs covering the seeds) is a common ingredient in some Middle Eastern dishes.

Traditionally, the fruits were boiled to make a wash to stop bleeding after childbirth. The berries, steeped in hot water, made a medicinal tea for treating diabetes, bowel problems and fevers. This tea was also used as a wash for ringworm, ulcers and skin diseases such as eczema. When chewed as a trail nibble, sumac fruits relieve thirst and leave a pleasant taste in the mouth.

Smooth sumac is a decorative, hardy species that provides an interesting fall and winter garden display. It does tend to sucker, though, so it can become invasive in the garden if not kept in check.

EDIBILITY: edible; dry but flavorful

FRUIT: Reddish, densely hairy, berry-like drupes, ¼ in long, in persistent, fuzzy clusters.

SEASON: Flowers May to July. Fruit ripens July to August, often remaining through winter.

DESCRIPTION: Deciduous shrub or small tree 3–10 ft tall, usually forming thickets. Twigs and leaves hairless; buds with whitish hairs. Branches exude milky juice when broken. Leaves compound, pinnately divided into 11–31 lance-shaped, toothed leaflets, 2–5 in long, bright red in fall. Flowers cream-colored to greenish yellow, about ⅛ in across, 5 fuzzy petals, in dense, pyramid-shaped clusters 4–10 in long. Grows in dry forest openings, on prairies and along fencerows, roadsides and in burned areas in eastern Washington (and King County) and north-eastern Oregon (occasionally in the Willamette and Tillamook valleys).

Smooth sumac (*R. glabra*)

Three-leaf sumac (*R. trilobata*) is a deciduous shrub growing to 8 ft tall. Leaves typically have 3 leaflets with wavy, somewhat lobed margins. Flowers white to yellow, appearing before the leaves on short, stiff branches. Fruit sticky, bright red-orange, hairy. Found in the Klamath Mountains in southwestern Oregon.

Three-leaf sumac (*R. trilobata*)

Indian Lemonade

Makes 8½ cups

Enhance this beautiful pink "lemonade" by adding ice cubes (or frozen blueberries) and green mint sprigs.

3 cups dried and crumbled sumac flower spikes
8 cups cold water · sugar to taste

Pick through the dried flower spikes to remove any dirt or debris. Crumble the red "berries" off the main spike and place them in a jug. Pour the cold water over the berries, mash the mixture with a wooden spoon or potato masher, then let sit for at least an hour. *Do not heat this mixture because it will alter the taste of the sumac.* Strain the liquid through a cheesecloth, jellybag or fine-mesh sieve, and add sugar to taste.

Blackberries *Rubus* spp.

Himalayan blackberry (*R. armeniacus*)

Blackberries and their relatives (raspberries, salmonberry, thimbleberry and cloudberry) are all closely related members of the genus *Rubus*. The best way to distinguish blackberry plants from raspberries is by looking at their fruits: if they are hollow like a thimble, they are raspberries, but if they have a solid core, they are blackberries.

Blackberries were traditionally gathered by indigenous peoples and are still widely enjoyed today. They were typically picked in large quantities and eaten fresh or stored (usually dried, either alone or with other fruit) for winter. A traditional method of eating blackberries was to combine them with other berries or with oil (sometimes whipped) and meat. Today, blackberries are enjoyed in many different ways: on their own, with cream or yogurt and sugar, in pies and sauces, as jam or jelly, or as drinks such as cordial, juice or wine.

Our native trailing blackberry is the first to ripen in early July, followed by the introduced Himalayan blackberry in early August, largeleaf blackberry and European blackberry in mid-August, and then cutleaf blackberry in September. Blackberry plants are widely cultivated across Canada for their delicious fruits; modern thornless cultivars are readily available for the home gardener. Blackberry-raspberry crosses such as loganberries and boysenberries are extremely flavorful and should be more popular and widely known than they are.

A Coast Salish origin story for trailing blackberry recounts that a jealous husband chased a woman up a tree. As the blood of the woman fell from the tree and reached the ground, the drops turned into blackberries. A purification rite of the same group involved scrubbing trailing blackberry stems across a person's body before a spirit dance.

The word "bramble" comes from the Old English *braembel* or *brom*, which means "thorny shrub."

EDIBILITY: highly edible; some of our tastiest fruit

FRUIT: Juicy red to black drupelets aggregated into clusters, falling from the shrub with the fleshy receptacle intact (i.e., blackberries have a solid core).

SEASON: Flowers May to July (sometimes into August in moist, shady or cool spots). Fruit ripens June to September.

DESCRIPTION: Prickly, perennial brambles. Canes often arching or trailing, 1½–15 ft long, usually biennial, often rooting at tips. Leaves alternate, compound. Flowers white to pinkish, 5-petaled.

Himalayan blackberry (*R. armeniacus*)

Cutleaf blackberry (*R. laciniatus*) grows to 10 ft tall or more, often as a thicket, generally evergreen. Stems ⅛–⅜ in thick, first ascending and arching, then sprawling or trailing, rooting at stem tips. Prickles flattened, stout, hooked. Leaflets 5, roughly egg-shaped, deeply lobed or toothed, sharp-pointed tip, smooth, green, slightly hairy above, grayish green and hairy below. Flowers pinkish to white, petals spreading, 3-lobed at tip. Fruits drupelets ⅜–⅝ in across, red ripening to very glossy black, globe- to egg-shaped, in clusters. Fruit has a distinctive taste, is much firmer than other blackberry species, ripens later and has a more pronounced core. Introduced from Eurasia. Found in western Washington and western Oregon, as well as the Columbia Gorge and the rolling hills of southern Washington and northern Oregon. Also called: evergreen blackberry.

Elmleaf blackberry (*R. ulmifolius*) is an upright to arched blackberry reaching 10 ft tall. Canes 5-angled, thornless to sparsely prickled, covered with a dense coat of short hairs. Flowers white to pink, in clusters of 10–60. Introduced from Europe. Grows mostly in California but found uncommonly in the Klamath Mountains and western Oregon.

European blackberry (*R. vestitus*) is similar to Himalayan blackberry but with straight instead of curved spines and a glandular-haired inflorescence. Leaf underside densely white-wooly. Scattered throughout Washington and western Oregon.

Himalayan blackberry (*R. armeniacus*) is a large, well-armored, perennial bramble to 15 ft tall. Canes biennial, 1 in in diameter at the base, covered in stout, curved spines, at first upright, then arching down to the ground where they may root. Second-year canes form thin, lateral branches. Leaves 3–8 in long, underside densely white-wooly, 5 palmately arranged leaflets on

Cutleaf blackberry (*R. laciniatus*)

Trailing blackberry (*R. ursinus*)

Elmleaf blackberry (*R. ulmifolius*)

first-year canes and smaller, fewer leaflets on second-year canes. Flowers white, 1 in wide, in clusters of 3–20 arising from two-year-old canes; stems of inflorescence often hairy but the hairs lack a glandular tip. Luther Burbank introduced this species from Armenia to Germany in about 1835, and then to America in 1885. It is spread readily by birds and reached our area around 1945. Found in open, disturbed sites from the Cascades westward in Washington and Oregon, as well as in southwestern Washington and northeastern Oregon. Considered an invasive species in Douglas-fir forests and particularly in Garry oak

Cutleaf blackberry (*R. laciniatus*)

meadows. Also called: *R. bifrons, R. procerus, R. discolor.*

Largeleaf blackberry (*R. macrophyllus*), introduced from Europe, is similar to Himalayan blackberry but has straight prickles. Leaves hairy, underside not covered in a dense mat of tangled, white hairs like Himalayan and European blackberry. Scattered in western Washington and Whitman County, Washington.

Trailing blackberry (*R. ursinus*) is a trailing shrub less than 2 ft tall with arching stems 15 ft long or more, rooting at shoot tips. Leaflets 3, deciduous to semi-evergreen (winter leaves take on a reddish green color). Found in thickets, dry, open forests, fields, streamsides and disturbed sites west of the Cascades and in northeastern Oregon. Also called: dewberry, Pacific blackberry.

Trailing blackberry (*R. ursinus*)

Himalayan blackberry (*R. armeniacus*)

Elmleaf blackberry (*R. ulmifolius*)

Trailing blackberry (*R. ursinus*)

Blackberry Syrup

Makes 3 x 1 cup jars

This fruity syrup makes a delicious warm or cold drink and is recommended for relieving the symptoms of the common cold. Add 1 Tbsp to 1 cup of hot water.

1 lb blackberries · 1 cup white wine vinegar · 1 cup sugar · 4 Tbsp honey

Place the clean fruit into a glass jar and pour the vinegar over top. Leave to stand for at least 24 hours, stirring and crushing the fruit regularly to extract the juices. Strain the liquid into a large saucepan and bring to the boil. Add the sugar, stirring until it's all dissolved. Add honey, stir well. Bring back to the boil, and boil hard for 5 minutes. Allow to cool completely. Pour into sterilized jars while still hot, and seal. Alternatively, you can pour the cooled liquid into ice cube trays in the freezer.

TIP

If you are pouring very hot liquid into a sterilized glass jar that has cooled, the sudden heat can cause the jar to crack. Avoid this problem by first pouring in a few tablespoons of the hot liquid and waiting 10 seconds for the heat to spread, then filling the rest of the jar.

Berry Blackberry Cordial

Makes approximately 4 x 1 cup jars if 8 cups of fruit are used

up to 8 cups freshly picked blackberries (or other juicy berries such as raspberries or thimbleberries, or a combination of berries) · white vinegar · sugar

Carefully pick through the fruit to remove any debris or insects. Be particularly wary of stink bugs, which are about ½ inch in size, green to brownish in color, flat-backed with a hard carapace, and emit a rank stench if bitten into: they will ruin the entire batch of cordial!

Place the berries in a large glass jar and crush somewhat firmly with a potato masher. Pour enough white vinegar into the jar to just barely cover the fruit mash (roughly an 8:1 ratio). Stir vigorously, put a firm lid on the jar, then let it sit somewhere warm out of direct sunlight for 1 week, stirring once a day.

After a week, strain the mixture overnight through a jellybag. *Resist squeezing it or you will push solids through the bag, resulting in a cloudy end-product with sediment.* The leftover fruit mash can be used in muffins or pancakes.

Measure out the resulting juice into a thick-bottomed saucepan and add 1 cup white granulated sugar for every 1 cup of juice. Slowly bring to the boil to fully dissolve the sugar. Let cool and place in washed, sterilized Mason-type jars for storage. Other glass containers with rubber-sealed tops also work well.

To make the cordial, mix the concentrate in a 6:1 ratio with cold water. Garnish with a sprig of fresh mint or some frozen whole berries.

Raspberries *Rubus* spp.

Arctic dwarf raspberry (*R. arcticus*)

Raspberries and their relatives (salmonberry, thimbleberry and cloudberry) are all closely related members of the genus *Rubus*. The best way to distinguish these plants from blackberries is by looking at their fruits: if they are hollow like a thimble, they are raspberries (or relatives), and if they have a solid core, they are blackberries.

The essence of summer, wild raspberries are one of our most delicious native berries and are fabulous fresh from the branch or made into pies, cakes, puddings, cobblers, jams, jellies, juices and wines. Because the cupped fruit clusters drop from the receptacle when ripe, these fruits are soft and easily crushed into a juicy mess when gathered. Raspberries were a popular and valuable food of indigenous peoples and were often gathered and processed into dried cakes either alone or with other berries such as salal for winter use. These cakes were reconstituted by boiling or were eaten as an accompaniment to dried meat or fish.

Raspberry-leaf tea and raspberry juice boiled with sugar have been gargled to treat mouth and throat inflammations.

The Coast Salish mixed wild raspberries with black twinberry and salal to make a purple stain. The fresh or dried leaves of these species have been used to make tea, and the flowers make a pretty addition to salads. Although strawberry-leaf raspberry fruits are delicious and juicy, they were not traditionally gathered in

Trailing wild raspberry (*R. pedatus*)

Western black raspberry (*R. leucodermis*)

Arctic dwarf raspberry (*R. arcticus*)

quantity because of their small size and the difficulty in picking them.

EDIBILITY: highly edible

FRUIT: Juicy red to black drupelets aggregated into clusters that fall from the shrub without the fleshy receptacle (i.e., raspberries and relatives have a hollow core).

SEASON: Flowers June to July. Fruit ripens July and August.

DESCRIPTION: Armed or unarmed, perennial shrubs or herbs, ½–12 ft tall. Leaves deciduous, lobed or compound (divided into leaflets). Flowers white to pink.

Arctic dwarf raspberry (*R. arcticus*) is a low, herbaceous plant (sometimes a bit woody at the base), to 6 in tall, with typically 3 leaflets and no prickles or bristles. Flowers pink to reddish. Fruits deep red to dark purple. Found in bogs, wet meadows and tundra. A northern species limited in our area to Okanogan County, Washington, where it is listed as critically imperiled. Also called: nagoonberry, arctic raspberry • *R. acaulis.*

79

Barton's raspberry (*R. bartonianus*)

Barton's raspberry (*R. bartonianus*) is a little-known, thornless raspberry with upright, hairy canes. Leaves usually less than 2 in long, underside hairless but stalks hairy. Flowers white, solitary. Endemic to Hells Canyon, it is found in thickets along tributaries to the Snake River and on protected canyonsides. Very limited range in our area, to the eastern edge of Wallowa County in northeastern Oregon. Also called: bartonberry.

Dwarf bramble (*R. lasiococcus*)

Dark raspberry (*R. nigerrimus*) is a native, upright to clambering bramble. Canes to 15 ft long, bluish green, with hooked, flattened prickles. Leaves green to bluish green, hairless on both sides, 5 leaflets (3 on flowering canes), the lower 2 leaflets sessile (stalkless). Flowers white, in loose clusters of 1–5. Fruit blackish, rough, relatively dry. Endangered, with a distribution limited to Whitman and Garfield Counties in southeastern Washington.

Dwarf bramble (*R. lasiococcus*) has slender, trailing stems to 6 ft long, with short, erect flowering branches to 5 in tall. Leaves 1–3 per erect branch, 3-lobed but not divided into leaflets, double-sawtoothed, 1–2½ in wide. This species is similar to trailing raspberry, both having leaves that appear 3-lobed, rather than the 5-lobed leaves of strawberry-leaf raspberry. Fruits drupelets, to ⅜ in wide, few to several in a cluster. Grows at middle to high elevations in the Olympic and Cascade mountain ranges. Also called: rough-fruit berry.

San Diego raspberry (*R. glaucifolius*) is a tangled bramble with narrow,

San Diego raspberry (*R. glaucifolius*)

Wild Berry Dressing

Makes about 2 cups

This dressing keeps well in the fridge for up to 10 days.

1 cup mixed tangy wild berries such as raspberries, thimbleberries or blackberries
½ cup olive oil • ¼ cup apple cider vinegar
1 tsp sugar • 2 cloves crushed garlic • 1 tsp salt

Crush the berries, then mix with all the remaining ingredients in a small jam jar. Screw on the lid tightly and shake vigorously.

lightly prickled canes. Leaves with usually 3 (sometimes 5) leaflets to 2 in long, shallowly lobed, toothed margins, white on undersides. Flowers white, in groups of 1 to few. Fruits red, slightly hairy. Grows in the mountains of California and as far north as Jackson County in the Oregon Siskiyous.

Snow raspberry (*R. nivalis*) is a trailing perennial with curve-prickled stems up to 6 ft long. Leaves mostly simple, occasionally with 3 leaflets, 1–2½ in long, smooth, hairless, petioles (leaf stalks) with curved prickles. Flowers pink, solitary or in pairs. Fruits red with large drupelets. Grows in the full shade of forested mountains at middle elevations. Found in the Cascades, Olympics and coastal mountains in western Washington and western Oregon.

Strawberry-leaf raspberry (*R. pedatus*) is a trailing herb with long, creeping stems (often moss-covered) to 3 ft long, rooting at nodes and producing short, erect stems usually less than 4 in tall, bearing flowers and 1–3 leaflets. Leaflets alternate, 3–5, coarsely toothed, no prickles or

Snow raspberry (*R. nivalis*)

Snow raspberry (*R. nivalis*)

bristles. Flowers solitary, on slender stalks, white, petals spreading or bent backward. Fruits dark or bright red clusters of flavorful, juicy drupelets (raspberries), sometimes only

Strawberry-leaf raspberry (*R. pedatus*)

1 drupelet per fruit. Found in low to subalpine elevations in bog forests, on streambanks and in moist, mossy forests in western and northern Washington (also Walla Walla County), and northwestern Oregon (but not the Willamette Valley). Also called: trailing wild raspberry, creeping raspberry, five-leaved bramble.

Trailing raspberry (*R. pubescens*) is a slender trailing, soft-hairy shrub to 2 ft tall, unarmed, with vegetative stems often more than 3 ft long, ascending at first, then reclining, rooting where nodes touch the ground. Leaflets alternate, long-stalked, 3–5 lobes, greenish and smooth-hairy above, paler beneath. Flowers white (rarely pinkish), 5-lobed, 1–3 on erect shoots 6–20 in long. Fruits dark red drupelets, to ³/₈ in

Trailing raspberry (*R. pubescens*)

across, smooth, several, not easily separating from spongy receptacle. Found on damp slopes and streambanks at middle elevations in northeastern Washington. Also called: dewberry, dwarf red blackberry.

Western black raspberry (*R. leucodermis*) has long, arching branches to 6 ft long. Stems highly prickly, with a whitish bloom. Leaves alternate, crinkly, deciduous, shiny and white beneath. Leaf stalks stout, prickly, broad-based, usually hooked. Flowers white to pink, clustered in leaf axils or at terminal end of stalk. Fruits "hairy"

Wild red raspberry (*R. idaeus*)

Wild red raspberry (*R. idaeus*)

raspberries, to ½ in wide, red (when unripe) to dark purple-black. Inhabits thickets, ravines, disturbed areas, forest edges and open woods throughout most of the forested parts of Washington and Oregon. Also called: blackcap, whitebark raspberry.

Wild red raspberry (*R. idaeus*) is an erect shrub to 6 ft tall, growing in thickets as it spreads by underground rhizomes. Fruits bright red, virtually identical to domesticated raspberries but smaller. Most common east of the Cascade Mountains, but also on the western slopes of the Cascades in Washington or northern Oregon. Found in thickets, open woods and fields, and on rocky hillsides. Also called: American red raspberry • *R. strigosis*.

Western black raspberry (*R. leucodermis*)

Trailing wild raspberry (*R. pedatus*)

Berry Fruit Leather

Makes 1 baking sheet of fruit leather

4 cups crushed berries (all one kind or a mix) • 2 cups apple sauce • ½ cup sugar

Mix the berries and sugar together in a pot on medium heat until the sugar is dissolved. Put the mixture through a food mill to remove any stems or seeds, then add the apple sauce and stir until well mixed. Grease a rimmed baking sheet and pour mixture in. Use a spatula to spread the mixture to an even thickness on the baking sheet, because the fruit leather will not dry evenly otherwise. Place in a food dehydrator or an oven at 150°F until firm to the touch and dry enough to peel off. Remove from the dehydrator or oven and let cool. Use scissors to cut the leather into strips. Cool the strips and store in an airtight container or Ziploc® bag.

Thimbleberry *Rubus parviflorus*

Thimbleberry (*R. parviflorus*)

Thimbleberry is one of the most delicious native berries you will encounter in the Pacific Northwest (and beyond!) and was highly regarded by all the Native American groups in its extensive range. The fruit is easy to pick as it can grow in large clusters and appears on the plant as a bright red treasure amid soft, maple-like leaves (no sharp prickles or spines!). The taste is somewhat like a raspberry but more intense and flavorful, with a sharper "tang." Once you've had thimbleberry pie, jam or tarts, you will never go back to its poorer cousin the raspberry!

The fruit, which is rather coarse and not overly juicy, dries and keeps well. Thimbleberries can also be gathered by cutting the stems of the unripe fruit,

which will ripen later in storage. Traditionally, these berries were gathered and mashed either alone or with other seasonal fruits such as salal, and then dried into cakes for winter use or trade. Tender shoots of this plant were traditionally harvested in April and early May and peeled to be eaten as a green vegetable.

The large, maple-like leaves of thimbleberry served many purposes for some indigenous peoples. They were used to whip soapberries, wipe the slime from fish, line and cover berry baskets and dry other kinds of berries. To make a temporary berry container, pick a leaf and snap off the stem. Fold the soft outer leaf edges together to form a funnel shape (the stem is at the narrow, bottom edge of this funnel, the leaf tips forming the wider top brim), then use the stem to prick through the 2 leaf folds where they overlap and "sew" the funnel together. If you still have a small hole at the bottom of your funnel, line this with part of another leaf. If you're out in the woods and have forgotten your toilet paper, thimbleberry leaves are soft and tough and make an excellent substitute.

EDIBILITY: highly edible

FRUIT: Bright red, shallowly domed (like a thimble), raspberry-like, hairy drupelets, in clusters above the leaves.

SEASON: Flowers late April to May. Fruit ripens July to August.

DESCRIPTION: Erect shrub, 1½–8 ft tall, main-stemmed, no prickles or spines, spreading by underground rhizomes and forming dense thickets. Bark light brown and shredding on mature stems, green on newer stems. Leaves alternate, large (6 in long), soft, fuzzy, maple-like, palmate with 3–7 lobes, toothed margins, finely hairy above and below. Flowers white, 5-petaled, to 2 in across, long-stemmed, in terminal clusters of 3–11. Found in moist, open sites such as road edges, shorelines and riverbanks, and in open forests at low to middle elevations.

Wild Berry Juice

Makes approximately 4½ cups

3 cups any sweet berries such as blueberries, thimbleberries or blackberries
2 cups water • sugar to taste

Pick over berries to remove any debris and place them in a saucepan with the water. Mash the mixture with a wooden spoon or potato masher, then simmer until berries are soft. Strain the mixture through a jellybag, fine-mesh sieve or cheesecloth, add sugar to taste, then let the juice cool before serving.

Salmonberry

Rubus spectabilis

Salmonberry (*R. spectabilis*)

Salmonberry fruits and shoots were popular foods for Native Americans along the coast. They were almost always eaten fresh, sometimes at feasts, because they are very juicy and do not preserve well. The shoots are still peeled and enjoyed raw, steamed or boiled as an early spring vegetable.

The flowers of this species are a magnificent rosy red to reddish purple color and make an excellent addition to an ornamental garden. Beware, though, of this plant's habit of spreading via underground rhizomes; it can become invasive.

These are one of the first flowers and fruits to come out in spring, and in numerous coastal languages, the month of May and sometimes the entire spring season is named after the salmonberry. Many Native American groups along the coast look to the salmonberry crop as an indicator of how good the Salmon run will be. The berries were traditionally eaten with grease, salmon or dried salmon eggs, and were sometimes mixed with other berries, sugar and a little water.

Swainson's thrush is called the "salmonberry bird" in many coastal Native American languages because it is associated with ripening salmonberries in Pacific Northwest native mythology.

EDIBILITY: highly edible

FRUIT: Large, raspberry-like, ranging when ripe from gold to ruby red to purplish black. Flavor varies greatly depending on plant and individual location.

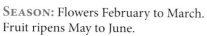

SEASON: Flowers February to March. Fruit ripens May to June.

DESCRIPTION: Robust, erect shrub, to 12 ft tall, growing in thickets from spreading rhizomes. Bark reddish brown to yellowish, shredding. Prickles present mostly on younger branches, sloughing off as bark matures. Leaves alternate, deciduous, sharply toothed, typically with 3 leaflets. Flowers 1–2 (rarely up to 4), pink to reddish, to 1 in wide, on short stems. Found in moist to wet forests, swampy or disturbed areas and along streambanks from low to middle elevations on both the eastern and western slopes of the Cascades and Olympics in Washington and west of the Cascades in Oregon.

Oregon-grapes   *Mahonia* spp.

Tall Oregon-grape (*M. aquifolium*)

These tart, juicy berries can be eaten raw but can be rather sour and intense, so they are more commonly used to make jelly, jam or wine. A frost increases the fructose content of the berries, making them sweeter and more palatable for fresh eating. Mashed with sugar and served with milk or cream, they make a tasty dessert. A refreshing drink can be made with mashed berries, sugar and water—the sweetened juice tastes much like Concord grape juice. Berry production can vary greatly from year to year, and the fruits are sometimes rendered inedible by grub infestations, so the eater should be wary of the potential for extra protein!

Plants of this genus contain the alkaloids berberine, berbamine, isocorydin and oxyacanthine, which stimulate involuntary muscles. The crushed plants and roots have antioxidant, antiseptic and antibacterial properties. Traditionally, they were used to make medicinal teas, poultices and powders for treating gonorrhea and syphilis, and for healing wounds and scorpion stings. The boiled, shredded root bark produces a beautiful, brilliant yellow dye.

Tall Oregon-grape is a decorative, tough, spiky, drought-tolerant and hardy plant that is often cultivated as an ornamental. It produces masses of bright yellow, fragrant flowers adored by pollinators early in spring, followed by tresses of decorative purple berries loved by birds and eventually a striking and lasting fall display of red leaves. Its sharp, spiky leaves also make it a good plant in areas where you may want to discourage pets or people from exploring.

Oregon-grape is the state flower of Oregon.

EDIBILITY: highly edible but very sour

FRUIT: Juicy, grape-like berries, tart and sour-tasting, about ½ in long, purplish blue with a whitish bloom.

SEASON: Flowers mostly from April to June (but occasionally in late winter!). Fruit ripens July to September.

California barberry (*M. pinnata*)

Tall Oregon-grape (*M. aquifolium*)

Dull Oregon-grape (*M. nervosa*)

DESCRIPTION: Perennial, evergreen shrubs to 10 ft tall. Outer bark rough, brown to grayish, with a striking canary or mustard yellow inner layer when scraped. Leaves leathery, holly-like, compound, pinnately divided into spiny-edged leaflets, glossy, dark green turning red or purple in winter. Flowers yellow, about ½ in across, forming elongated, whorled clusters.

California barberry (*M. pinnata*) is an evergreen shrub similar to tall Oregon-grape. It usually grows 1–5 ft tall with upright, unbranched, smooth-barked stems. Leaves divided into 3–13, often overlapping leaflets with spiny margins. Flowers yellow, in

89

Dull Oregon-grape (*M. nervosa*)

Creeping Oregon-grape (*M. repens*)

Creeping Oregon-grape (*M. repens*)

dense clusters of 25–50. Berries blue, ¼ in wide. Restricted in our area to Curry County, Oregon.

Creeping Oregon-grape (*M. repens*) is a creeping, broadleaf evergreen shrub 4–20 in tall, spreading by both underground rhizomes (root-bearing stems) and surface suckers. Leaves alternate, with 5–7 dull or shiny leaflets, bluish green with a white bloom underneath. Grows in open forests, scrublands and grasslands at low to montane elevations in eastern Washington and all but the northwestern corner of

Oregon. Also called: holly grape • *Berberis repens.*

Dull Oregon-grape (*M. nervosa*) grows 4–32 in tall. Leaves with 9–19 pairs of dull (rather than shiny) leaflets, opposite from a common stem, with whitish bloom underneath. Grows in moist to dry forests and on open slopes at low to montane elevations on both slopes of the Cascades and west to the coast, as well as northeastern Washington and northeastern Oregon. Also called: Cascade Oregon-grape, Cascade barberry • *Berberis nervosa.*

Tall Oregon-grape (*M. aquifolium*) grows 1½–9 ft tall. Leaves with 5–11 leaflets (usually broadly spaced), shiny above, not whitened beneath, with a prominent central vein. Flowers in both upright clusters and hanging racemes. Grows in dry forests at low to montane elevations in all but the driest parts of Washington and western Oregon, including Umatilla and Union Counties. Also called: Oregon grape, holly-leaved barberry • *Berberis aquifolium.*

WARNING: *High doses of Oregon-grape can cause nosebleeds, skin and eye irritation, shortness of breath, sluggishness, diarrhea, vomiting, kidney inflammation and even death. Pregnant women should not use this plant because it may stimulate the uterus.*

Tall Oregon-grape (*M. aquifolium*)

Salal and Oregon-grape Jelly

Makes 16 x 1 cup jars

8 cups salal berries • 8 cups Oregon-grape berries • ¼ cup lemon juice
1 packet powdered pectin • 5 cups sugar

Place salal and Oregon-grape berries in a thick-bottomed saucepan on medium heat. Crush and stir the berries and simmer until the juice is released, about 10 minutes. Strain through a cheesecloth or fine-mesh sieve to separate the juice. *Do not squeeze the cloth or force the mix through the sieve because it will cause sediments to run into the juice, resulting in a cloudy jelly.*

Measure out 4 cups of the resulting juice into a thick-bottomed saucepan. Add the lemon juice and pectin, stirring until the pectin is thoroughly dissolved. Add the sugar, stirring constantly, and bring to a rolling boil. Hold the mixture at the boil for 3 minutes, being careful to stir the bottom so that the jelly does not stick or burn.

Meanwhile, prepare 16 x 1 cup jars and lids (wash and sterilize jars and lids, and fill jars with boiling water; drain just before use).

Remove from heat, skim off any foam (the impurities coming out of the liquid) and pour into the hot, sterilized jars. Carefully wipe the jar edges to ensure they are clean and dry, then place the lids on and tighten the metal screw bands. Place jars in a cool area. You will know that the jars have sealed when you hear the snap lids go "pop."

Currants   *Ribes* spp.

Red-flowering currant (*R. sanguineum*)

Currants are commonly distin-guished from gooseberries by their lack of spines. They were eaten by many Native American groups, and are common and widespread throughout our area. All are considered edible, but some are tastier than others, and some (such as wax currant and sticky currant) are considered emetic in large quantities and best avoided. Currants are high in pectin and make excellent jams and jellies—either alone or mixed with other fruit—that are deli-cious with meat, fish, bannock or toast. Historically, currants were also mixed with other berries and used to flavor liqueurs or fermented to make delicious wines, but raw currants tend to be very tart.

Wax currant has been described as tasteless, dry and seedy, bitter and similar to dried crab apples. Golden currant is one of the most flavorful and pleasant-tasting currants. Some species, such as stink currant, have a skunky or lemony smell and flavor when raw but are delicious cooked.

In Europe, currant juice is taken as a natural remedy for arthritic pain. Black currant seeds contain gamma-linoleic acid, a fatty acid that has been used in the treatment of migraine headaches, menstrual problems, diabetes, alcoholism, arthritis and eczema.

Some native peoples believed that northern black currant had a calming effect on children, so sprigs were often hung on baby carriers. Currant shrubs growing by lakes were seen by Native Americans as indicators of fish; in some legends, when currants dropped into the water, they were transformed into fish.

Red-flowering currant is commonly sold at plant nurseries as a decorative native shrub, with flowers ranging in color from pure white to dark red.

The name "currant" comes from the ancient Greek city of Corinth, where a small purple grape (*Uva corinthiaca*) is grown and sold commercially as a "currant." The genus name *Ribes* comes from the Arabic *ribas*, which means "acidic," referring to the taste of the fruit. We have nearly 30 *Ribes* species in our area.

For more information on closely related species, see the sections on gooseberries (pp. 98–103) and prickly currants (pp. 104–05).

EDIBILITY: edible, ranging from sweet to tart to skunky

FRUIT: Tart, juicy berries (currants), often speckled with yellow, resinous dots or bristling with stalked glands. Fruit color varies from bright red to green to black, as do sweetness and juiciness depending on the species and individual location.

SEASON: Flowers April to July. Fruit ripens July to August.

DESCRIPTION: Erect to ascending deciduous shrubs, 3–10 ft tall, without spines at nodes but often dotted with yellow, crystalline resin-glands that have a sweet, "tomcat" odor. Leaves alternate, 3- to 5-lobed, usually rather maple-like. Flowers small, about $1/4–3/8$ in across, 5 petals, 5 sepals, in elongating clusters in spring.

Crater Lake currant (*R. erythrocarpum*)

Crater Lake currant (*R. erythrocarpum*) is a trailing perennial. Stems hairy, spineless, rooting. Leaves 1–2 in long, 3–5 lobed, with hairy and gland-covered surfaces. Flowers yellowish orange, saucer-shaped, in clusters of few to several (to 15). Berries red, $1/3–3/8$ in long. Grows in forests and glades, and on rocky slopes in the Cascade Mountains of southern and central Oregon. Of conservation concern.

Cultivated red currant (*R. rubrum*) is a small, unarmed bush usually less than 5 ft tall. New stems slightly pocked with small glands, older growth smooth. Leaves 1–2 in wide, 5-lobed, smooth above, with slightly hairy veins on the underside. Flowers green to greenish brown, saucer-shaped, in 8–20-flowered racemes. Berries bright red, smooth, sour.

93

Distinguished from red swamp currant by its smooth-stemmed berries (those of red swamp currant have stalked glands). Found in gardens and on old homestead sites. Introduced from Europe to Puget Sound, Pend Oreille Valley and the Portland area. Also called: red garden currant.

European black currant (*R. nigrum*) is a cultivated fruit introduced from Europe and is grown occasionally in British Columbia and Wallowa County, Oregon. Stems 3–6 ft tall, sparsely hairy but otherwise smooth. Flowers green, cup-shaped, densely hairy, in hanging clusters. Fruit black, round, mostly smooth with some glands.

Golden currant (*R. aureum*) grows 3–9 ft tall and is named for its showy, bright yellow flowers, not its smooth fruits, which range from black to red and sometimes yellow-orange. Leaves with 3 widely spreading lobes and few or no glands. Inhabits streambanks and wet grasslands to dry prairies and open or wooded slopes throughout eastern Washington and eastern Oregon. Lewis and Clarke were taught to eat golden currants by Sacagawea in 1805.

Mapleleaf currant (*R. acerifolium*) grows to 4 ft tall. Stems covered with fine hairs and stalked glands. Flowers pink, broadly bowl-shaped, in hanging

Cultivated red currant (*R. rubrum*)

clusters of 7–15. Fruit smooth, black. Grows from middle elevations to treeline along streambanks and on rockslides, open ridges and meadowlands on mountainsides in the Olympics, Cascades, northeastern Washington and Oregon's Blue Mountains. Also called: *R. howellii*.

Northern black currant (*R. hudsonianum*) grows to 5 ft tall. Leaves relatively large, maple-like, resin-dotted on lower surface. Flowers white, saucer-shaped, in elongated clusters of 6–12. Berries shiny, resin-dotted, black, strong-smelling,

Golden currant (*R. aureum*)

Golden currant (*R. aureum*)

European black currant (*R. nigrum*)

Red swamp currant (*R. triste*) is an unarmed, reclining to ascending shrub to 5 ft tall. Flowers small, reddish or greenish purple, saucer-shaped, in drooping clusters of 6–15; flower stalks jointed, hairy, glandular. Fruits bright red, smooth, sour but palatable. Found in moist, coniferous forests and swamps, along streambanks and on montane, rocky slopes.

often bitter-tasting. Found in wet woods and on rocky slopes in eastern Washington and eastern Oregon.

Red-flowering currant (*R. sanguineum*) is an erect, unarmed shrub, 3–9 ft tall, with crooked stems and reddish brown bark. Flowers are a beautiful and distinctive rose color (varying from pale pink to deep red), rarely white, $^1/_4$–$^3/_8$ in long, in erect to drooping clusters of 10–20 or more. Berries round, glandular-hairy, blue-black with a white, waxy bloom, $^1/_4$–$^3/_8$ in across, insipid and seedy. Inhabits dry to moist, open forests and openings at low to middle elevations on both slopes of the Cascades and westward.

Red swamp currant (*R. triste*)

Northern black currant (*R. hudsonianum*)

Northern black currant (*R. hudsonianum*)

Sticky currant (*R. viscosissimum*) is a loosely branched shrub to 6 ft tall, with erect to spreading stems. Leaves 3- to 5-lobed, heart-shaped at the base, 1–5 in wide, glandular-sticky. Flowers white or creamy, in clusters of up to 16. Berries bluish black, hairy, glandular. Grows in moist to dry forests and woodlands at montane to subalpine elevations in eastern Washington and in all but coastal Oregon.

Stink currant (*R. bracteosum*) is a more or less erect, unarmed, straggly, deciduous shrub growing to 9 ft tall. All parts of the plant are covered with round, yellow glands that smell sweet-skunky or catty. Leaves alternate, 2–8 in wide, maple-like, deeply 5- to 7-lobed, sweet-smelling when crushed. Flowers white to greenish

Trailing black currant (*R. laxiflorum*)

white, 20–40 in long, erect clusters 6–12 in long. Berries blue-black with a whitish bloom, edible, taste varying from unpleasant to delicious. Found in moist to wet places, including woods, streambanks, floodplains, shorelines, thickets and avalanche tracks, at low to subalpine elevations throughout western Washington and western Oregon.

Trailing black currant (*R. laxiflorum*) is a trailing, spreading plant, occasionally vining, with branches growing along the ground and usually less than 3 ft tall. Flowers greenish white to reddish purple. Fruits purplish black with stalked, glandular hairs and a waxy bloom. Inhabits clearings, disturbed sites such as avalanche tracks and roadsides, and moist forests at low to middle elevations. Found in western Washington and Oregon.

Mapleleaf currant (*R. acerifolium*)

Stink currant (*R. bracteosum*)

Wax currant (*R. cereum*) grows to 3 ft tall. Leaves shallowly lobed, fan-shaped, glandular on both sides. Flowers white to pinkish, in small clusters of 2–6. Berries red, smooth to glandular-hairy. Found on dry slopes and rocky places east of the Cascades in Washington but on both slopes of the Cascades and eastward as you move toward southern Oregon.

Wax currant (*R. cereum*)

Sticky currant (*R. viscosissimum*)

Wolf's currant (*R. wolfii*)

Sticky currant (*R. viscosissimum*)

Wolf's currant (*R. wolfii*) is an upright to slightly spreading shrub to 12 ft tall. Stems finely hairy with black glands. Flowers green to pink, cup-shaped, in, upright to spreading, finely haired racemes of 7–25. Berries round, 1/8–1/2 in wide. This is a rare currant found only in moist meadows and forests at moderate elevations in Garfield and Asotin Counties in southeastern Washington and in Wallowa County in northeastern Oregon. Of conservation concern.

97

Gooseberries *Ribes* spp.

Northern gooseberry (*R. oxyacanthoides*)

Although gooseberries and currants are closely related species, they are generally different in that gooseberries have spines or prickles on their stems (currants are not thus "armed") and gooseberry fruits are usually borne in small clusters or singly (currants occur in elongated clusters, generally with more than 5 fruits). However, because common names are inconsistent, some "gooseberries" don't have spines and some "currants" do!

All gooseberries are edible raw, cooked or dried, but flavor and sweetness vary greatly with species, habitat and season. All are high in pectin and make excellent jams and jellies, either alone or mixed with other fruits. Gooseberries can be eaten fresh and are also delicious in baked goods such as pies. Traditionally, these berries were eaten with grease or oil, or were mashed

(usually in a mixture with other berries) and formed into cakes that were dried and stored for winter use. Dried gooseberries were sometimes included in pemmican, and dried gooseberry and bitterroot cakes were sometimes a trade item. Because of their tart flavor, gooseberries can be used much like cranberries. They make a delicious addition to turkey stuffing, muffins and breads. Timing is important, however, when picking these fruits. Green berries are too sour to eat, and ripe fruit soon drops from the branch. Sometimes green berries can be collected and then stored so that they ripen off the bush. Eating too many gooseberries can cause stomach upset, especially in the uninitiated.

Because of the large number of species and wide distribution of gooseberries, there is a very large spectrum of uses for these plants. Gooseberries were commonly eaten or used in teas for treating colds and sore throats, which may be related to their high vitamin C content. Teas made from gooseberry leaves and fruits were given to women whose uteruses had slipped out of place after too many pregnancies. Gooseberry tea was also used as a wash for soothing skin irritations such as poison-ivy rashes and erysipelas (a condition with localized inflammation and fever caused by a streptococcus infection). Gooseberries have strong antiseptic properties, and extracts have proven effective against yeast (candida) infections.

Picking this fruit can be a formidable task because of the often-thorny stems. Indeed, gooseberry thorns can be so large and strong that they were historically used as needles for probing boils, removing splinters and even applying tattoos! The name "gooseberry" comes from an old English tradition of stuffing a roast goose with the berries.

EDIBILITY: edible

FRUIT: Smooth, purplish (when ripe) berries, about ³⁄₈ in across.

SEASON: Flowers May to June. Fruit ripens July to August.

DESCRIPTION: Erect to sprawling deciduous shrubs with spiny branches. Leaves alternate, maple-like, 3- to 5-lobed, about 1–2 in wide. Flowers whitish to pale greenish yellow, tubular, to ½ in long, with 5 small, erect petals and 5 larger, spreading sepals, in clusters of 1–4 in leaf axils.

Canyon gooseberry (*R. menziesii*) is a heavily armored shrub 3–6 ft tall. Stems hairy, covered with prickles, with 3½ in long spines at the nodes. Leaves ⅝–1 in wide, smooth above, hairy on the underside. Flowers white-pink, hanging singly or in pairs. Berries reddish purple and hairy with gland-tipped bristles. Found along the western slopes of the Coast Range in southwestern Oregon.

Coastal black gooseberry (*R. divaricatum*) is an erect to spreading shrub growing to 6 ft tall. Branches arching, the stems not prickly but with 1–3 stout spines on each node. Bark grayish, smooth. Leaves small,

Canyon gooseberry (*R. menziesii*)

maple-like, with 3–5 lobes. Flowers white to more commonly red to reddish green, drooping, in clusters of 2–4. Berries round, smooth, purplish black when ripe, skin translucent, with the dried, brown flowerhead attached at the bottom end of the ripe fruit. Found in open woods, meadows, moist clearings and on hillsides at low

Coastal black gooseberry (*R. divaricatum*)

Coastal black gooseberry (*R. divaricatum*)

elevations mainly in western Washington and western Oregon. Also called: spreading gooseberry.

Desert gooseberry (*R. velutinum*) is a densely branched, spreading shrub reaching 6 ft tall. Stems smooth to hairy, with 1–3 spines at the nodes. Leaves ¼–1 in across, leathery, with surfaces ranging from smooth to finely hairy and glandular. Flowers white or light yellow, solitary or in clusters of 2–3. Ovaries usually densely hairy. Berries yellow maturing to purple, smooth to hairy. Found only in Whitman and Asotin Counties in Washington and scattered across south-central and eastern Oregon.

Ground gooseberry (*R. binominatum*) mostly trails along the ground with the occasional stem reaching upward to 3 ft. Stems hairy with 3 spines at the nodes. Leaves 1–2 in wide, hairy on both sides. Flowers white to green, solitary or hanging in clusters of 2–3. Found in southwestern Oregon at moderate to subalpine elevations. Of some conservation concern.

Hupa gooseberry (*R. marshallii*) is a medium-sized shrub 3–6 ft tall.

Sticky gooseberry (*R. lobbii*)

Stems arched, fuzzy, with 3 spines at the nodes. Leaves 1–1½ in wide, slightly hairy but without glands. Flowers in hanging clusters of 1–3, with maroon sepals surrounding bright yellow, tubular petals. Berries dark red with prickles. Found in high

Ground gooseberry (*R. binominatum*)

forests in Josephine and Jackson Counties in southwestern Oregon. Also called: Marshall's gooseberry.

Mountain gooseberry (*R. oxyacanthoides* ssp. *irriguum*) is a subspecies of northern gooseberry and is differentiated by having distinctive long, glandular flower stalks and a broad calyx tube (the structure between the petals and the flower stalk) with lobes (sepals) that are longer than the tube. Found in far-eastern Washington and the northeastern corner of Oregon.

Northern gooseberry (*R. oxyacanthoides*) is an erect to sprawling shrub to 5 ft tall. Branches bristly, often with 1–3 spines to ⅜ in long at the nodes; bristles absent or few between nodes. Twigs gray to straw-colored, older bark whitish gray. Inhabits wet forests, thickets, clearings, open woods and exposed, rocky sites in eastern Washington and northeastern Oregon. Also called: smooth gooseberry • *R. hirtellum, R. setosum.*

101

Desert gooseberry (*R. velutinum*)

Shinyleaf gooseberry (*R. cruentum*) is an upright shrub 1½–4 ft tall. Stems hairy, with 1–3 spines at the nodes and no prickles between the nodes. Leaves ½–2¼ in long, 3–5 rounded lobes, hairy stem. Leaf surfaces range from smooth to hairy to wooly. Flowers maroon, tubular, hanging alone in or pairs. Fruit purple, round, hairy and spiny. Grows on dry, rocky slopes in southwestern Oregon on both sides of the Cascades and Siskyous. Also called: spiny-fruited gooseberry, Sierra gooseberry • *R. roezlii* var. *cruentum*.

Slender-branched gooseberry (*R. niveum*) is an upright shrub, 4–9 ft tall with gray to reddish brown bark and stout spines ⅓–½ in long at the nodes. Leaves broadly rounded to kidney-shaped, 1–2 in wide, with 3–5 round-toothed lobes and fine hairs on both surfaces. Flowers white or pale green, tubular, hanging in clusters of 3–4. Berries round, ⅜–½ in wide, dark blue, sour-tasting. Found in thickets along streams and on open

hillsides in the southeastern corner of Washington in Whitman, Garfield and Asotin Counties and in north-central and eastern Oregon. Also called: snow currant.

Spring gooseberry (*R. watsonianum*) is an ascending to upright shrub 3–6 ft tall. Stems covered with gray hairs and stalked glands, with 1–3 spines at the nodes. Leaves 1–2 in wide, fuzzy, with stalked glands. Flowers white to

Shinyleaf gooseberry (*R. cruentum*)

pinkish, solitary or in clusters of 2–3. Berries reddish, densely covered with yellowish spines. Found in the mountains on both slopes of the Cascades to central Oregon, in mid-elevation forest openings, ridges and canyons.

Sticky gooseberry (*R. lobbii*) is a straggly shrub 1½–3 ft high. Stems covered with soft, sticky hairs (hence the common name), with clusters of 3 slender spines at each node. Bark reddish brown, shredding with age. The fruits are up to 1 in diameter, the largest of our native gooseberries, resembling cultivated gooseberries in size and flavor. Found from lowland valleys and streambanks to open or wooded montane slopes sporadically throughout Washington and western Oregon. Also called: gummy gooseberry.

Stream gooseberry (*R. oxyacanthoides* ssp. *cognatum*) is a subspecies of northern gooseberry and has sepals densely covered with fine hairs (vs. slightly hairy to hairless as in mountain gooseberry). Found in north-central and southeastern Washington and northeastern Oregon.

White-stemmed gooseberry (*R. inerme*) is similar to coastal black

Slender-branched gooseberry (*R. niveum*)

gooseberry but has white to pinkish petals (vs. often reddish in coastal black gooseberry) less than $\frac{1}{16}$ in long (vs. $\frac{1}{16}-\frac{1}{8}$ in long in coastal black gooseberry). Stems lose their bristles with age and have 1–3 (if any) spines at the nodes. Flowers hang alone or in clusters of 2–5. Berries greenish or reddish purple to grayish black. Grows in foothill and montane forests in eastern Washington and non-coastal Oregon.

Spring gooseberry (*R. watsonianum*)

White-stemmed gooseberry (*R. inerme*)

Prickly Currants *Ribes* spp.

Prickly black currant (*R. lacustre*)

Despite the prickly and strongly irritating stems of these plants, the fruit is quite palatable when ripe and makes delicious jams and pies (either alone or mixed with other fruit) for those who survive the spikes. Prickly currants are an unusual group of species in that they have characteristics common to both currants and gooseberries. Like gooseberries, they are covered in many sharp prickles that are also highly irritating. Like currants, their fruit hangs in large clusters of generally more than 5 berries.

Although the flavor of prickly currants is sometimes described as insipid, Native Americans often used them for food. The berries were traditionally eaten fresh off the bush, cooked, stored in the ground for winter use or sometimes dried. Dried prickly currants were occasionally included in pemmican, and they make a tasty addition to bannock, muffins and breads.

Prickly currants may be boiled to make tea or mashed in water and fermented with sugar to make wine. The leaves, branches and inner bark of prickly black currant were used to produce a menthol-flavored tea, sometimes called "catnip tea." To make this tea, the spines were singed off, and the branches (fresh or dried) were steeped in hot water or boiled for a few minutes. Prickly black currant fruits were traditionally rolled on hot ashes to singe off their soft spines before eating. Some native peoples considered the spiny branches (and by extension, the fruit) to be poisonous. However, these dangerous shrubs could also be useful as their thorny branches were thought to ward off evil.

EDIBILITY: edible

FRUIT: Shiny, red or purplish black berries, ¼ in wide, bristly with glandular hairs, hanging in drooping clusters.

SEASON: Flowers in April. Fruit ripens May to August.

DESCRIPTION: Erect to spreading, deciduous shrubs with spiny, prickly branches. Leaves alternate, 3- to 5-lobed, maple-like. Flowers reddish to maroon, saucer-shaped, about ¼ in wide, in hanging clusters of 7–15.

Mountain prickly currant (*R. montigenum*) is similar to prickly black currant but has smaller leaves (generally ½–1 in wide) that are glandular-hairy on both sides and bright red berries. Grows on rocky montane, subalpine and alpine slopes on the east side of the Cascades. Also called: alpine prickly currant.

Prickly black currant (*R. lacustre*) is an erect to spreading shrub, 1½–6½ ft tall, covered with numerous small, sharp prickles and larger, thick spines at leaf nodes. Bark on older stems cinnamon-colored. Leaves large (⅛–¼ in wide), hairless to slightly hairy. Berries dark purple. Found in moist woods and along streambanks to drier forested slopes and subalpine ridges. Also called: prickly currant, swamp gooseberry, bristly black currant, swamp black currant.

Prickly black currant (*R. lacustre*)

Mountain prickly currant (*R. montigenum*)

105

Serviceberries *Amelanchier* spp.

Also called: saskatoon, juneberry, shadbush

Serviceberry (*A. alnifolia*)

These sweet fruits were and still are extremely important to many indigenous peoples across North America. Indeed, there is a well-documented history of extensive landscape management through fire, weeding and pruning to encourage the healthy growth of these important species. Traditionally, large quantities of serviceberries were harvested and stored for consumption during winter. They were eaten fresh, dried like raisins or mashed and dried into cakes for winter use or trade. Some indigenous peoples steamed serviceberries in spruce bark vats filled with alternating layers of red-hot stones and fruit. The cooked fruit was mashed, formed into cakes and dried over a slow fire. These cakes could weigh as much as 15 lbs each!

Dried serviceberries were the principal berries mixed with meat and fat to make pemmican and were commonly added to soups and stews. Today, they are popular in pies, pancakes, puddings, muffins, jams, jellies, sauces, syrups and wine, much like blueberries.

Historically, serviceberry juice was taken to relieve stomach upset, the green fruit was boiled to make drops to treat earaches and dried berries were used to make eye drops. The fruit was given to mothers after childbirth for afterpains and was also prescribed as a blood remedy. The berry juice, which can stain your hands when picking, makes a good purple dye.

Serviceberries are excellent ornamental, culinary and wildlife shrubs. They are hardy and easily propagated, with beautiful white blossoms in spring, delicious fruit in summer and colorful, typically scarlet leaves in fall. There are a number of improved garden cultivars available for superior fruit production in the home garden.

EDIBILITY: highly edible

FRUIT: Juicy, berry-like pomes, ¼–½ in across, red at first, ripening to purple or black, sometimes with a whitish bloom.

SEASON: Flowers April to June. Fruit ripens July to August.

DESCRIPTION: Shrub or small tree to 20 ft tall, often forming thickets. Bark smooth, gray to reddish brown. Leaves alternate, coarsely toothed on upper half, 1–2 in long, oval to nearly round, yellowish orange to reddish brown in autumn. Flowers white, petals slightly twisted, in short, leafy clusters near branch tips. Grows at low to middle elevations on prairies, in thickets, meadows and open woods, and on hillsides and dry, rocky shorelines throughout our region, particularly east of the Cascades.

Serviceberry (*A. alnifolia*)

WARNING: *The fresh leaves and seeds contain poisonous, cyanide-like compounds. However, cooking or drying destroys these toxins.*

Utah serviceberry (*A. utahensis*)

Serviceberry (*A. alnifolia*) is a spreading shrub 5–15 ft tall. Young branches have reddish bark that becomes gray with age. Leaves 1–2 in long, oval, with distinctive sawtoothed tips. Flowers white, in compact clusters. Fruits purple, smooth. Found throughout our region but more common east of the Cascades where the fruit also tastes much better. • Plants west of the Cascades are sometimes divided into several varieties with the common name saskatoon serviceberry. Var. *humptulipensis* and var. *alnifolia* both have thin, hairy leaves and flower petals less than ½ in long. Var. *humptulipensis* has only 4 styles per flower and is found only in western Washington, whereas var. *alnifolia* has 5 styles per flower and is found east of the Cascades. Var. *semiintegrifolia* and var. *cusickii* both have flower petals greater than ⅝ in long. Var. *semiintegrifolia* is found west of the Cascades and has grayish, wooly-topped fruit, whereas var. *cusickii* (also called Cusick's serviceberry) is found east of the Cascades and has smooth, purple fruit.

Dwarf serviceberry (*A. pumila*)

Dwarf serviceberry (*A. pumila*) is small shrub with thick, hairless, leathery leaves and white flowers with petals less than ⅝ in long. Fruit purple, usually smooth, occasionally with a few hairs on top. Found sporadically in the Cascades, Blue Mountains, Siskiyous and southeastern Oregon.

Utah serviceberry (*A. utahensis*) is a hairy shrub usually less than 10 ft tall. Young branches and undersides of leaves covered with wooly hairs. Fruit sometimes hairy. Found on seasonally wet hillsides and in washes from sagebrush desert to mid-elevation mountains. Uncommon in Washington on the eastern slope of the Cascades and Whitman County; more abundant in Oregon, where it is found in the Blue Mountains, Siskiyous and southeastern parts of the state.

Utah serviceberry (*A. utahensis*)

Serviceberry Squares

¼ cup butter • ⅔ cup brown sugar
1 tbsp vanilla • 1 large egg, beaten
1 cup flour • 1 tsp baking powder
½ tsp salt • ½ tsp cinnamon
½ cup FROZEN serviceberries (or wild blueberries)
½ cup chopped walnuts or almonds

Preheat oven to 350°F. Melt the butter gently in a saucepan, then remove from heat and stir in sugar, vanilla and beaten egg. Mix dry ingredients in a bowl. Make a shallow well in the middle, and gradually mix in wet ingredients from the saucepan. When it's well mixed, add frozen serviceberries and chopped nuts. Pour into an 8-inch pan and bake for 35 minutes. Remove from oven and cool before cutting into squares.

Pemmican

Makes 6 cups

Pemmican uses the same drying temperature as the fruit leather on p. 83, so make both recipes at the same time!

3 Tbsp salted butter • 3 Tbsp brown sugar
¼ tsp dried powdered ginger
¼ tsp ground cloves • ¼ tsp ground cinnamon
4 cups serviceberries or blueberries
4 cups beef jerky, chopped into small pieces
½ cup chopped almonds, walnuts or hazelnuts (optional)
½ cup sunflower seeds (optional)

Gently heat butter with sugar and spices in a heavy-bottomed pot. Mash berries and add to pot. Simmer, stirring constantly, for about 5 minutes. Let mixture cool, then mix in jerky and nuts and/or seeds. Grease a rimmed baking sheet, spread mixture evenly on sheet and let dry overnight in oven at 150°F.

Dogwoods *Cornus* spp.

Red-osier dogwood (*C. sericea*)

The fruits of Pacific dogwood, red-osier dogwood and brown dogwood are definitely bitter-tasting to modern-day palates. Although Pacific dogwood produces fruit of an attractive red color that looks like it should be delicious, the taste is mealy and bitter. However, despite their bitterness, the berries of red-osier dogwood were gathered by some Native Americans in northeastern Washington in late summer and autumn and eaten immediately. They were also occasionally stored for winter use, either alone or mashed with sweeter fruits such as service-berries, and in more modern times with sugar. The Kootenai make a dish

called "sweet and sour," which is a mixture of red-osier dogwood fruit, a sweet berry such as service-berry and a bit of sugar. Red-osier dogwood fruit can be cooked when fresh to release the juice, which purportedly makes a refreshing drink when sweetened. Some people separated the stones from the mashed flesh and saved them for later use. They were then eaten as a snack, somewhat like peanuts are today. However, the stones should not be eaten in large quantities, and the taste is probably not worth the effort involved. Pacific dogwood and brown dogwood were not eaten by any Native American groups, but the pretty red

Pacific dogwood (*C. nuttallii*)

Pacific dogwood (*C. nuttallii*)

berries of Pacific dogwood were used ceremonially by the Hoh and Quileute. All of our dogwoods are attractive ornamental trees with good wildlife and aesthetic value.

EDIBILITY: Red-osier dogwood is edible with caution; Pacific dogwood and brown dogwood are not recommended and are potentially toxic.

FRUIT: White, brown or red, berry-like drupes, small but growing up to ½ in across, in open to tight clusters of at least 20. Attractive but mealy, hard and bitter; 2 of our 3 species are not considered edible and are perhaps best left to the birds.

SEASON: Flowers May to June. Fruit ripens late summer.

DESCRIPTION: Upright shrubs to small trees with opposite branching. Leaves smooth-margined with arching veins that release latex when torn.

Brown dogwood (*C. glabrata*) is a shrub or small tree less than 20 ft tall. Stems brown to reddish purple. Leaves gray-green, 1–2 in long. Fruit

Pacific dogwood (*C. nuttallii*)

white to bluish white with smooth stones. Grows in moist places. A southwestern species limited in our area to the Siskiyous. Also called: smooth dogwood.

Pacific dogwood (*C. nuttallii*) is a small deciduous tree, erect to sprawling, to 65 ft tall. Bark blackish brown, smooth, becoming finely ridged with age. Branches opposite, gray-purplish when young. Leaves opposite, simple, pointed, toothless, with leaf veins following the smooth leaf edges toward the tip, greenish above, white to gray below, turning red in autumn. Flowers small, yellowish green or red, radially symmetrical with 4 sepals, 4 petals and 4 stamens, all attached at the top of the ovary. In clusters of flowers of about 75, to 1 in wide, subtended by 4–7 showy, white or pinkish-tinged bracts. (Note that to the common observer, these showy bracts appear as the large "petals" of a giant flower, whereas the tiny true flowers appear as a decorative center to that main display.) Grows in moist, well-drained soils in the shade of coniferous trees on both slopes of the Cascades. Inhabits a wide range of habitats from moist valley bottoms to just below higher-elevation timberline.

Red-osier dogwood (*C. sericea*) has 2 subspecies that grow in our area:

Pacific dogwood (*C. nuttallii*)

Pacific dogwood (*C. nuttallii*)

Pacific dogwood (*C. nuttallii*)

ssp. *occidentalis* grows west of the Cascades, whereas ssp. *sericea* (differentiated mainly by having fruit with smooth rather than rough stones) grows east of the Cascades. Erect to sprawling, deciduous shrub or small tree, slender and branching in form, to 18 ft tall. Twigs and branches opposite, shiny, smooth, bright green to red when young (the more sun exposure on the stem, the brighter the red color), becoming brown when older. Leaves opposite, simple, pointed, toothless, with veins following the smooth leaf edges toward the tip, greenish above, white to grayish below, becoming red in autumn. Flowers small, clustered, 1–2 in wide, without showy bracts, from May to August. Fruits berry-like drupes, pea-sized, to $^3/_8$ in across, white (sometimes bluish), containing large, flattened stones. Whiter fruits, though bitter, are reportedly less so than bluer-tinged ones. Grows on moist sites, shores and in thickets throughout our area. Also called: western red osier, creek dogwood • *C. stolonifera*.

Red-osier dogwood (*C. sericea*)

Red-osier dogwood (*C. sericea*)

Red-osier dogwood (*C. sericea*)

Red-osier dogwood (*C. sericea*)

WARNING: *All parts of these species are considered toxic, especially if consumed in large quantities.*

Bunchberry *Cornus unalaschkensis*

Also called: western bunchberry, Canada dogwood, dwarf dogwood • *C. canadensis*

Bunchberry (*C. unalaschkensis*)

The bright scarlet-orange fruit of this woodland plant looks like it should be poisonous, but it is actually quite edible. However, opinions of the flavor range from insipid to sweet, flavorful and similar in taste to the highly regarded salal berry. In British Columbia, the Bella Coola and Sechelt gathered bunchberries to eat fresh, either on their own or with eulachon grease, and more recently enjoyed them with granulated sugar. In our area, they are neither as abundant nor were as widely used by Native Americans, and a few groups even considered them inedible.

The berries are plentiful wherever the plant grows, and it is easy to gather a quantity with minimal effort. They can be eaten raw as a trail nibble and are also said to be good cooked in puddings. However, each drupe contains a hard seed, so those with mature dental work should be wary. Bunchberries, usually mixed with other fruits, can be used whole to make sauces and preserves or cooked and strained to make beautiful, scarlet-colored syrups and jellies.

Bunchberry is reported to have anti-inflammatory, fever-reducing and pain-killing properties (rather like

DESCRIPTION: Perennial herb, 2–8 in tall, spreading from a rhizome. Leaves wintergreen-like, 1–3 in long, opposite, in groupings of 2–6, spaced so tightly that appear whorled. Flowers tiny, in a dense clump at the center of 4 white to purple-tinged, petal-like bracts (exactly like miniature flowers of the dogwood tree), forming single, flower-like clusters about 1 in across. Grows in cool, moist woods and damp clearings at low to subalpine elevations; commonly found on rotting stumps and logs. Also called: *C. canadensis* (this name is now applied to a different species that doesn't grow in our area).

mild aspirin) but without the stomach irritation and potential allergic effects of salicylates. The plant has a history of being used to treat headaches, fevers, diarrhea, dysentery and inflammation of the stomach or large intestine. The berries were eaten and/or applied in poultices to reduce the potency of poisons. They were also chewed and the resulting pulp applied topically to soothe and treat burns. Bunchberries have historically been steeped in hot water to make a medicinal tea for treating paralysis or boiled with tannin-rich plants such as common bearberry or commercial tea to make a wash for relieving bee stings and poison-ivy rash. Native peoples used a tea made with the entire plant to treat aches and pains, lung and kidney problems, coughs, fevers and seizures.

EDIBILITY: edible

FRUIT: Bright orange-red, berry-like drupes, 1/4–3/8 in wide, in dense clusters at stem tips (hence the common name "bunchberry"), nestled in a whorl of leaves. Drupes have yellowish pulp and 1 seed.

SEASON: Flowers May to August. Fruit ripens July to August.

AMAZING: *This plant spreads its relatively heavy pollen grains using an interesting "explosive pollination" mechanism. When the pollen is ripe and ready to be released, an antenna-like trigger in the flower releases, rapidly springing the 4 pollen-laden anthers violently upward together in a snapping motion and catapulting the pollen grains far up into the air for dispersal.*

Huckleberries *Vaccinium* spp.

Evergreen huckleberry (*V. ovatum*)

Huckleberries are delicious and well worth identifying and eating. Despite huckleberries and blueberries being separated by 2 distinct sets of common names, botanists do not make a formal distinction between these fruits. Both huckleberries and blueberries tend to have a delightful combination of sweet and tart flavors. Huckleberry fruit is typically blackish or red and glossy, whereas blueberries are generally blue with a whitish bloom.

Huckleberries can be used like domestic blueberries, eaten fresh from the bush, added to fruit salads, cooked in pies and cobblers, made into jams and jellies or crushed and used in cold drinks. They are also delicious in pancakes, muffins, cakes and puddings.

Dried huckleberry leaves and berries also make excellent teas. Bears and other wildlife relish huckleberries.

On the west coast, many Native Americans considered evergreen huckleberries to be the tastiest, and they traditionally traveled considerable distances to collect them. These berries were eaten fresh or dried for winter use and trade. Although they ripen in early autumn, evergreen huckleberry fruit can remain on the plants until December, and some reports claim that they taste even better after a frost.

Some people consider black huckleberry the most delicious and highly prized berry in western North America, especially in the Cascades and eastward. Black huckleberries are

Grouseberry (*V. scoparium*)

Evergreen huckleberry (*V. ovatum*)

cranberries but are milder and sweeter and are excellent eaten fresh. If you have enough willpower to gather some in a bucket to take home rather than eating them all in situ, these berries make particularly good jams and pies. You can use red huckleberries wherever cranberries are called for in a recipe, either sweet or savory. Red huckleberry shrubs make an excellent addition to the home garden and do well in moist, shady locations that many other plants reject. An established red huckleberry specimen will reward the homeowner with a pretty display of delicate green leaves in

collected in large quantities even today in open, subalpine sites such as old burns, and they are sold commercially in some regions.

Huckleberries are considered good for the liver by some Native Americans and are eaten as a ceremonial food to ensure health and prosperity for the coming season. Red huckleberries are traditionally eaten fresh, dried or made into cakes, or mixed with grease or oil to preserve them for winter use, gifts or as a trade item. The berries are mashed and formed into cakes or spread loosely on mats for drying. Later, they are reconstituted by boiling them either alone or with other foods.

Red huckleberry fruit is tart and delicious, and in a good patch, it is easy to harvest these berries in large quantities. They taste similar to

LITERARY REFERENCES: *The small, dark, rather insignificant fruit of the huckleberry became a metaphor in the early part of the 19th century for something humble or minor. This later came to mean somebody inconsequential, an idea that was the basis for Mark Twain's famous character, Huckleberry Finn. In an 1895 interview, Twain revealed that he wanted to establish the boy as "someone of lower extraction or degree than Tom Sawyer." The modern word "huckleberry" is an American distortion of the British "whortleberry," a name that originated from the Anglo Saxon words* wyrtil, *meaning "little shrub," and* beri *meaning "berry."*

spring and a delicious crop of decorative, bright berries in late summer. It will attract wildlife (competition for the berries!), and at the end of the year, provide a striking winter display with pinkish-colored stems that look lovely in winter floral arrangements. More recently, the winter branches of red huckleberry have become popular as greenery in the florist trade.

The berries of grouseberry are sweet and wonderful, but their small size makes picking them rather time consuming. Try using a (clean) comb to rake the berries into a basket, hat or other container to speed up this process. This species can grow quite abundantly in alpine areas, so a little persistence will yield a good haul. Try to get there early, though—this berry is a favorite food of chipmunks, red and gray foxes, squirrels, skunks and many bird species such as blue, spruce and ruffed grouse, as well as ptarmigans, bluebirds and thrushes. The plants themselves are a favorite browse for mule deer, bears, moose and mountain goats. Tough competition, indeed!

EDIBILITY: highly edible, among the season's best!

FRUIT: Berries, to ³⁄₈ in across, range in color from red to purple to black. All *Vaccinium* species have a small "crown" at the bottom end of the berry, which is a residual left over from the flower that was pollinated to form the fruit.

SEASON: Flowers April to June. Fruit ripens July to September.

DESCRIPTION: Deciduous or evergreen shrub, 1–10 ft tall. Leaves alternate, 1–2 in long. Flowers various shades of pink, round to urn-shaped, ¼ in long, single, nodding on slender stalks.

Black huckleberry (*V. membranaceum*) is a deciduous shrub to 5 ft tall, with purplish black berries. Branches at most slightly angled, yellowish green or reddish green when young, becoming grayish brown with age. Leaves with serrated margins and glandular undersides. Grows in dry to moist forests at montane to subalpine elevations on open or wooded slopes throughout Washington and Oregon. Also called: thinleaf huckleberry, black mountain huckleberry.

Evergreen huckleberry (*V. ovatum*) is an erect, bushy shrub to 12 ft tall. Branches at most slightly angled, greenish when young becoming brown with age. Leaves evergreen, egg-shaped, 1–2 in long, shiny, leathery, paler beneath. Flowers to ¹⁄₃ in long, in clusters of 3–10. Berries deep purplish

Black huckleberry (*V. membranaceum*)

Black huckleberry
(*V. membranaceum*)

Vaccinium species

Common names can be confusing, especially with the large variety of Vaccinium *species we have in our area. Blueberries, cranberries and huckleberries are all closely related plants in this genus. In North America, there are approximately 35 different* Vaccinium *species (there are 14 in our region!), but hybridization is common in the genus, so the true number of varieties is probably greater. As a general rule,* Vaccinium *species with blue fruits are called blueberries, and taller shrubs with fruits that aren't blue are called huckleberries. Shorter* Vaccinium *species with red berries and a distinctive tart flavor are commonly referred to as cranberries. However, common names do not necessarily follow this botanical protocol. For example, highbush cranberry (*Viburnum edule*) is in the honeysuckle family and is not a "true" cranberry at all, despite its red color and tart flavor. Rest assured, though, that none of these species are poisonous, and they are all delicious!*

black or occasionally blue, shiny, 1/8–1/4 in wide. Grows at low to montane elevations in dry to moist forests in coastal areas. Also called: California huckleberry.

Grouseberry (*V. scoparium*) is a low, creeping, broom-like perennial shrub to 1 ft tall. Branches numerous, squarish, slender, pale green, strongly angled, growing so closely together that they can be bundled and used as a broom once the leaves have fallen in autumn. Leaves deciduous, alternate, ovate, 1/4–1/2 in long, thin, finely toothed. Flowers tiny, 1/8 in long, 4 petals fused into urn-shaped blooms, pink, solitary. Berries single, bright red, 1/4 in across, smelling tantalizingly like huckleberry jam when ripe! Inhabits open, coniferous forests on foothill, montane and subalpine slopes from medium to high elevations in Washington, particularly in lodgepole pine areas. Also called: grouse whortleberry, littleleaf huckleberry.

Red huckleberry (*V. parvifolium*) is a deciduous shrub to 12 ft tall. Branches green, strongly angled, often pink in winter. Leaves light green, alternate, oval, to 1/8 in long, often remaining on

Red huckleberry (*V. parvifolium*)

119

the plant through mild coastal winters. Flowers bell to urn-shaped, greenish white to pinkish yellow, ⅜ in long. Berries up to ⅜ in across, bright pink to reddish orange or red, not ripening all at once. Grows in dry to moist, coniferous forests and on forest edges at low to medium elevations and in montane zones west of the Cascades, most abundantly on the coast.

False huckleberry (*Menziesia ferruginea*) has small, urn-shaped flowers that look very similar to those of *Vaccinium* species. The fruit of this plant is a small, many-seeded capsule. Sometimes there are small, pink, berry-like "fruits" on the undersides of the leaves, but these "berries" are actually the fruiting bodies of a fungus (*Exobasidium vaccinii*). Although all parts of this plant are poisonous, these fungal "berries" are apparently edible. According to Tsimshian legend, this fungus (which they ate) is the snot of

Red huckleberry (*V. parvifolium*)

Henaaksiala, a mythical creature that stole corpses. Found on both slopes of the Cascades and westward into the Olympics and the Coast Range. Scattered distribution in northeastern and southeastern Washington.

False huckleberry (*Menziesia ferruginea*)

False huckleberry (*Menziesia ferruginea*)

Tom's Huckleberry Pie

Makes 1 double-crust pie

The secret to a good, crispy pastry that is not tough and "dough-like" is to keep all your ingredients cool. Warm ingredients melt the small fat globules, causing them to mix too completely with the flour and resulting in chewy pastry. Leftover pastry trimmings make excellent little tartlets if rolled out again and put into the bottom of muffin tins, and filled with any extra huckleberry filling or jam out of the fridge.

Pastry
2 cups all-purpose flour · ½ tsp salt
⅔ cup vegetable shortening · ⅓ cup COLD milk

Filling
3 cups red or black huckleberries · ¼ cup water or freshly squeezed orange juice
1 cup granulated white sugar · 3 Tbsp cornstarch

For the pastry, sift the flour and salt together, then use 2 butter knives or a pastry cutter to cut the shortening into the flour mixture until the butter pieces are the size of small peas. *Avoid using your hands at this stage because their warmth will cause the butter to melt.* Gradually stir in the cold milk, then quickly shape the dough into 2 balls. Wrap them in plastic film, press into flat rounds and refrigerate immediately.

For the pie filling, mash the huckleberries with the water and put into a medium saucepan. Mix the cornstarch and sugar together and stir well into the COLD berries and water. *Do not heat the berries and water first because the cornstarch will cook prematurely and go all nasty and lumpy!* Bring mixture slowly to the boil, stirring constantly to avoid the cornstarch sticking or becoming lumpy. Simmer until noticeably thick, about 4 to 5 minutes, then take the saucepan off the burner.

Preheat oven to 350°F. Take the pastry out of the fridge, spread a thin layer of flour on a work surface, and roll the pastry until it is approximately ¼-inch thick. Place it into an 8-inch pie tin, cutting any extra off from around the edges. Next, roll out the second half of your dough into a similar-sized round. Fill the pastry shell with the huckleberry mixture, then carefully place the second round on top. Gently push the edges of the top and bottom pastry crusts together (you may need to lightly wet one edge to get it to stay together), and prick a few holes with a fork in the top to allow steam to escape during cooking. Bake for approximately 50 minutes.

Grouseberry (*V. scoparium*)

Blueberries   *Vaccinium* spp.

Bog blueberry (*V. uliginosum*)

Blueberry fruit tends to be blue, hence the common name of this group of plants. The fruit is generally sweet, rather than tart/sour (cranberries) or sweet/tangy (huckleberries). The group is sometimes divided into two, with the taller and bluer-fruited species being called "blueberries" and the ground-hugging, darker-fruited species called "bilberries," but we use this folk taxonomy loosely and refer to them collectively as "blueberries."

Wild blueberries are simply delicious! Rich in vitamin C and natural antioxidants, blueberries are both beautiful to look at and good for you to eat. These sweet, juicy berries can be eaten fresh from the bush, added to fruit salads, cooked in pies, tarts and cobblers, made into jams, syrups and jellies, or crushed and used to make juice, wine, tea and cold drinks. Blueberries also

make a wonderful addition to pancakes, muffins, cakes and puddings, as well as to savory treats such as chutneys and marinades. Cascade bilberry and bog bilberry are two of our best-tasting species.

Numerous blueberry species were widely used by Native Americans, either fresh, dried singly or mashed and formed into cakes. To make dried cakes, the berries were cooked to a mush to release the juice, spread into

Alaska blueberry (*V. alaskaense*)

slabs and dried in the sun or near a fire on a rack made from wood, rocks or plant materials. Often, the leftover juice was slowly poured onto the drying cakes to increase their flavor and sweetness.

Because blueberries grow close to the ground, they can be difficult and time consuming to collect, so some Native American groups developed a method of combing them from the branches with a salmon backbone or wooden comb or rake. Although this method was efficient, it resulted in baskets full of both berries and small, hard-to-pick-out blueberry leaves. The savvy solution developed for this problem was to place a wooden board at a medium angle and slowly pour the berry/leaf mix from the top of the board. The berries (which are round) would roll down the board to a basket waiting below, but the leaves (which are flat) would stick to the board and stay put. After 2 to 3 rollings, the picker would end up with a basket of pure berries with significantly less effort than would have been required to pick the leaves out individually. The only drawback to this method was that the occasional green berry also got included, but these were easily removed by hand.

Although most people associate blue-berries only with delicious fruit, there are many historical medicinal uses for other parts of this wide-ranging plant. Blueberry roots were boiled to make medicinal teas that were taken to relieve diarrhea, gargled to soothe sore mouths and throats, or applied to slow-healing sores. Bruised roots and berries were steeped in gin, which was

taken freely (as much as the stomach and head could tolerate!) to stimulate urination and relieve kidney stones and water retention. Blueberry-leaf tea and dried blueberries have historically been used like cranberries to treat diarrhea and urinary tract infections.

Common bilberry contains anthocy-anosides, which are said to improve night vision. These compounds are most concentrated in the dried fruit, preserves, jams and jellies. Their effect, however, is said to wear off after 5 to 6 hours. Anthocyanins may reduce leakage in small blood vessels (capil-laries), and blueberries have been suggested as a safe and effective treatment for water retention during pregnancy and for hemorrhoids, varicose veins and similar problems. They have also been recommended to reduce inflammation from acne and other skin problems and to prevent

Velvetleaf blueberry (*V. myrtilloides*)

cataracts. People suffering from hypoglycemia or diabetes have used blueberry-leaf tea to stabilize and reduce blood-sugar levels, and to reduce the need for insulin. The leaf or root tea of common bilberry is reported to flush pinworms from the body. Blueberry leaves were sometimes dried and smoked, and the berries have been used to dye cloth a navy blue color.

Velvetleaf blueberry (*V. myrtilloides*)

EDIBILITY: highly edible

FRUIT: Berries round, 3/16–3/8 in wide, bluish, usually with a grayish bloom, growing in clusters.

SEASON: Flowers May to July. Fruit ripens July to September.

DESCRIPTION: Low, often matted shrubs. Leaves thin, oval, 3/8–1 in long. Flowers whitish to pink, nodding, urn-shaped, to 1/4 in long.

Alaska blueberry (*V. alaskaense*) is very similar to oval-leaved blueberry (and is treated as such by many taxonomists), but has flowers that appear before the leaves (vs. with the leaves in oval-leaved blueberry), flowers that are usually wider than long (vs. longer than wide in oval-leaved blueberry) and leaves with

coarse, stiff hairs along the underside midrib (vs. bare-ribbed and smooth-margined in oval-leaved blueberry). Flowers April to May. Grows at low to subalpine elevations in mesic to moist forests and openings in the Washington Cascade and Olympic ranges.

Bog blueberry (*V. uliginosum*) is a low, spreading, deciduous, perennial shrub, 4–24 in tall (but as short as 1 in in areas of heavy snow where the shrub is crushed flat each winter). Branches rounded, brownish. Leaves alternate, 1 in long, fuzzy to smooth, elliptic to

WARNING: *Blueberry leaves contain moderately high concentrations of tannins, so they should not be used continually for extended periods of time.*

Fruit Popsicles

Makes 8 to 12 popsicles

Easy and a popular treat for adults and kids at any time of the year!

4 cups wild berries · 1 cup plain yogurt or light cream
1 cup white sugar · 1 cup orange or other fruit juice (optional) .

Blend all ingredients together, pour into the compartments of a popsicle maker and place in freezer until frozen.

Cascade bilberry (*V. deliciosum*)

oval, narrow and broadest toward the tip, dull whitish green, untoothed, with pronounced netted veins on the underside. Flowers solitary or in pairs, 4–5 lobed, white or pinkish, urn-shaped, to $\frac{1}{4}$ in long. Berries dark blue to blackish with a whitish bloom, to $\frac{3}{8}$ in across. Inhabits low-elevation bogs and boggy forests along the coast, as well as subalpine heath and alpine slopes and tundra in the Cascades. Also called: bog bilberry • *V. occidentale*.

Alaska blueberry (*V. alaskaense*)

Cascade bilberry (*V. deliciosum*) is a low, often matted and densely branched shrub 6–16 in tall. Stems greenish brown, minutely hairy or smooth, inconspicuously angled. Leaves to 1 in long, pale green with a whitish bloom beneath. Fruits blue to blue-black, $\frac{1}{4}$–$\frac{1}{3}$ in wide, almost globe-shaped, single or in pairs, ripening early July to September. Inhabits dry to moist forests, open areas and bogs at middle to subalpine elevations in the Olympics and Cascades. Also called: Cascade blueberry, Rainier blueberry, blueleaf huckleberry.

Common bilberry (*V. myrtillus*) is a low, many-branched shrub to 1 ft tall. Stems strongly angled, greenish brown, minutely hairy. Leaves alternate, $\frac{1}{2}$–1 in long, light green, elliptic-lanceolate to egg-shaped, sharply toothed margins, strongly veined, prominent rib on lower surface.

125

Highbush blueberry (*V. corymbosum*)

Flowers ⅛ in across, pinkish, in leaf axils, solitary, on nodding stalks, blooming May to July. Fruit to ⅜ in across, globe-shaped, dark red to bluish black without a whitish bloom, ripening July to October. Easy to confuse with grouseberry (*V. scoparium*), p. 119, but common bilberry has a more open habit with minutely hairy branches that are thicker and less numerous (those of grouseberry are more broom-like), as well as being slightly larger with darker-colored fruit. Bilberries are similar in appearance and taste to blueberries, but bilberry fruit tends to have darker flesh and the bushes grow lower to the ground. Note that the common name "whortleberry" also refers to black alpine bearberry (*Arctostaphylos alpina*). Inhabits dry, mesic forests and wooded montane and subalpine slopes mostly east of the Cascades in Washington, but scattered throughout Oregon. Also called: low bilberry, whortleberry • *V. oreophilum*.

Dwarf bilberry (*V. cespitosum*) is a low, usually matted shrub, 4–12 in tall. Branches rounded, yellowish to reddish. Leaves light green, finely toothed. Flowers 5-lobed, producing berries singly in leaf axils from August to September. Grows at middle to high elevations in moist meadows and on rocky ridges throughout our region. Also called: dwarf blueberry.

Highbush blueberry (*V. corymbosum*) is a low shrub 4–20 in tall. Twigs green, round-angular, with lines of hairs. Leaves ½–3 in long, ½–1 in wide, smooth, leathery, margins sawtoothed. Flowers in clusters of 2–10. Berries to ½ in wide, blue to black with a whitish bloom. Introduced from eastern North America, where it has escaped cultivation and grows in swamps and along sandy lakesides; mostly found in the Puget Sound area but also shows up along the coast and in the Willamette Valley.

Oval-leaved blueberry (*V. ovalifolium*) is a tall shrub, to 6 ft tall, with hairless, angled branches. Leaves entire or only sparsely toothed. Berries purple with a whitish bloom, ripening early July to September. Grows in dry

Dwarf bilberry (*V. myrtillus*)

Dwarf blueberry (*V. caespitosum*)

to moist forests, openings and bogs at low to subalpine elevations in the Cascade, Olympic and Coast ranges south to the Siuslaw and Umpqua National Forests in Oregon; also documented in the Blue Mountains.

Velvetleaf blueberry (*V. myrtilloides*) is a low shrub to 1 ft tall, with velvety branches, especially when young. Fruits bright blue, ripening August to October. Grows in dry forests, barrens and bogs at montane elevations. Restricted in our area to Okanogan County, Washington.

Oval-leaved blueberry (*V. ovalifolium*)

Blueberry Cobbler

1 cup flour · 2 Tbsp sugar · 1½ tsp baking powder
¼ tsp salt · 1 tsp grated lemon zest · ¼ cup butter
1 beaten egg · ¼ cup milk · 2 Tbsp cornstarch
½ cup sugar · 4 cups fresh blueberries (or huckleberries)

Preheat oven to 425°F. Sift together all the dry ingredients. Mix wet ingredients together, then pour slowly into the dry mix, stirring until just moistened.

Mix cornstarch and sugar together, and toss with the fruit. Pour this mixture into the bottom of an 8 x 10-inch glass or ceramic baking dish (avoid metal dishes because the acid in the fruit might turn it rusty and impart a nasty flavor to the cobbler). Drop the topping in spoonfuls on top of the fruit, covering the surface as evenly as possible (some exposed areas of fruit are fine). Bake uncovered for 25 minutes or until light brown.

Bog cranberry (*V. oxycoccos*)

Like many other species of wild berries with domesticated counterparts, wild cranberries are small but packed with a flavor that seems disproportionate to their size. The tartness of cranberries gives them an enviable versatility for sweet, sour and savory dishes. Who could imagine Thanksgiving dinner or many juices, desserts or baking without them? These berries, which also have a long history of medicinal use in treating kidney and urinary ailments, are touted today for their strong antioxidant properties. (Note that bush-cranberries and highbush cranberries (*Viburnum* spp.), though tart and cranberry-tasting, are in the honeysuckle family and are treated in a separate account on pp. 154–59.)

Cranberries can be very tart, but they make a refreshing trail nibble. They are also delicious in jams and jellies, and they can be crushed or chopped to make tea, juice or wine. A refreshing drink is easily made by simmering crushed berries with sugar and water or, more traditionally, by mixing cranberries with maple sugar and cider. Cranberry sauce is still a favorite with meat or fowl, and the berries add

Bog cranberry (*V. oxycoccos*)

a pleasant zing to fruit salads, pies and mixed-fruit cobblers. Cranberries are also a delicious addition to pancakes, muffins, breads, cakes and puddings.

Firm, washed berries keep for several months when stored in a cool place. They can also be frozen, dried or canned. Native Americans sometimes dried cranberries for use in pemmican, soups, sauces and stews. Some tribes stored boiled cranberries mixed with oil and later whipped this mixture with snow and fish oil to make a dessert.

Freezing makes cranberries sweeter, so they were traditionally collected after the first heavy frost. Because they remain on the plants all year, cranberries can be a valuable survival food rich in vitamin C and antioxidants. These low-growing berries are difficult to collect, so they were sometimes combed from the branches with a salmon backbone or wooden comb.

Cranberry juice has long been used to treat bladder infections. Research shows that these berries contain arbutin, which prevents some bacteria from adhering to the walls of the bladder and urinary tract and causing infection. Cranberry juice also increases the acidity of the urine, thereby inhibiting bacterial activity, which can also relieve infections. Commercial cranberry juice or cocktail blends are not appropriate for this treatment, however, as the juice is very processed, often diluted with other juices and highly sweetened (sugars feed the problem bacteria and can make an existing condition worse). Increased acidity can also lessen the urinary odor of people suffering from incontinence. The tannins in cranberries have anti-clotting properties and can reduce the amount of plaque-causing bacteria in the mouth, so are thus helpful in preventing gingivitis. Research has shown that cranberries contain antioxidant polyphenols that may be beneficial in maintaining cardiovascular health and immune system function, as well as preventing tumor formation. Although some of these compounds have proved extraordinarily powerful in killing certain types of human cancer cells in the laboratory, their effectiveness when ingested is unknown. There is also evidence that cranberry juice may prevent the formation of kidney stones. Cranberries were traditionally prescribed to relieve nausea, ease cramps in childbirth and quiet hysteria and convulsions. Crushed cranberries were used in poultices for wounds, including poison-arrow wounds. The red

Bog cranberry (*V. oxycoccos*)

pulp that is left after the berries have been crushed to make juice can be used to make a red dye. A related species, lingonberry (*V. vitis-idaea*), is popular in Sweden as a digestive aid and is used in jams, jellies, pies and other baking, as well as in juice, wine, liqueur, herbal teas and as "cranberry sauce." The Inupiat Inuit used a wrapped cloth containing mashed berries to treat sore throats and crushed the berries to treat itchy skin conditions such as chickenpox or measles. The mashed fruit, mixed with oil, was fed to convalescents to help them recover their strength.

EDIBILITY: highly edible

FRUIT: Berries bright red (sometimes purplish) when ripe, ¼–⅜ in wide, tart and delicious, said to be best after the first frost and can be foraged for when the snow melts in spring—if the wildlife have left any behind!

SEASON: Flowers June to July. Fruit ripens August to September and may persist on plants throughout winter.

Cultivated cranberry (*V. macrocarpon*)

DESCRIPTION: Dwarf, low-spreading, deciduous shrubs, mostly less than 8 in tall, often trailing. Flowers small, nodding, pinkish.

Bog cranberry (*V. oxycoccos*) has slender, creeping stems, with small (mostly less than ½ in long), pointed, glossy leaves. Flowers distinctive, 4 petals separated almost to the base and strongly curved backward (like

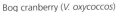

Bog cranberry (*V. oxycoccos*)

Bog cranberry (*V. oxycoccos*)

Cranberry Chicken

Serves 5

3 lbs chicken · ¼ cup flour · ½ tsp salt
¼ cup cooking oil · 1½ cups fresh cranberries
½ cup sugar · 1 Tbsp grated orange zest
½ cup fresh orange juice · ¼ tsp ground ginger

Cut chicken into serving-sized pieces, and coat with flour and salt. Heat oil in a cast-iron skillet. Add chicken pieces and brown on both sides, being careful to cook the chicken fully. Combine remaining ingredients in a saucepan, bring to the boil and pour it over the chicken in the skillet. Cover skillet, reduce heat and simmer 30 to 40 minutes until chicken is tender.

little shooting stars), appearing terminal on stems. Fruit deep red, round, about ³⁄₁₆–³⁄₈ in wide, ripens July to August. Predictably inhabits bogs. Also called: small cranberry · *Oxycoccus oxycoccos, O. quadripetalus, O. microcarpus.*

Cultivated Cranberry (*V. macrocarpon*) is a trailing plant with stems ascending 2–6 in. Generally larger than bog cranberry but best distinguished by flower characteristics. Flowers midstem (not terminal). Bracts (the leaves on the flowering stalk) ⅛–³⁄₈ in long, more than halfway up the hairy flowering stalk. Fruit red, ³⁄₈–⅝ in wide. Introduced from northeastern North America for cultivation, this species has escaped to coastal bogs. Also called: *Oxycoccus macrocarpus.*

Cultivated cranberry (*V. macrocarpon*)

False-wintergreens *Gaultheria* spp.

Slender false-wintergreen (*G. ovatifolia*)

The small, sweet berries of this species are delicious and can be eaten fresh, served with cream and sugar or cooked in sauces. Their flavor improves after freezing, so they are at their best in winter following the first frost (even from under the snow if you are persistent!) or in spring when they are plump and juicy. The young leaves are an interesting trailside nibble or can be added to salads, as well as used to make a strong, aromatic tea that is said to make a good digestive tonic. The wintergreen flavor can be drawn out if the bright red leaves are first fermented.

The berries were historically mixed with teas and used to add fragrance and flavor to liqueurs. Occasionally, large quantities were picked and dried like raisins for winter use. During the American Revolutionary War, wintergreen tea was a substitute for black tea (*Camellia sinensis*). The berries were traditionally soaked in brandy, and the resulting extract was taken to stimulate appetite, as a substitute for bitters.

All false-wintergreen species contain methyl salicylate, a close relative of aspirin, which relieves aches and pains.

These plants were widely used in the treatment of painful, inflamed joints resulting from rheumatism and arthritis (see Warning). Studies suggest that oil of wintergreen is an effective painkiller, and it also has numerous commercial applications. It provides fragrance to various products such as toothpastes, chewing gum and candy, and is used to mask the odors of some organophosphate pesticides. It is a flavoring agent (at no more than 0.04 percent strength) and an ingredient in deep-heating sports creams. The oil is also a source of triboluminescence, a phenomenon in which a substance produces light when rubbed, scratched or crushed. The oil, mixed with sugar and dried, builds up an electrical charge that releases sparks when ground, thus producing the Wint-O-Green Lifesavers optical phenomenon. To observe this, look in a mirror in a dark room and chew the candy with your mouth open!

Slender false-wintergreen (*G. ovatifolia*)

Hairy false-wintergreen
(*G. hispidula*)

Hairy false-wintergreen (*G. hispidula*)

EDIBILITY: highly edible

FRUIT: Mealy to pulpy, fleshy, berry-like capsules with a mild wintergreen flavor.

SEASON: Flowers May to June. Fruit ripens late August into September.

DESCRIPTION: Delicate, creeping, evergreen shrublets. Leaves leathery, small. Flowers white to greenish or pinkish.

Alpine false-wintergreen (*G. humifusa*) has glossy leaves $3/8$–1 in long, rounded to blunt at the tip. Flowers pinkish or greenish white, 5-lobed, $1/8$ in wide, with a hairless calyx. Berries scarlet, pulpy, $1/4$ in wide, drier and not as palatable as other *Gaultheria* species. Grows in moist to wet, subalpine to alpine meadows in the Cascades, Olympics, Wallowa and Blue ranges. Also called: alpine wintergreen, creeping wintergreen.

Hairy false-wintergreen (*G. hispidula*) is similar to alpine false-wintergreen but has tiny, stiff, flat-lying, brown hairs on its stems and lower leaf

surfaces. Leaves very small (less than $3/8$ in long). Flowers tiny ($1/16$ in wide), 4-lobed. Berries white, small (generally less than $1/4$ in across), on very short stalks, persisting through fall. Grows in cold, wet bogs and coniferous forests in montane and subalpine zones. Associated with acidic soils, often growing in mosses under conifers or on rotting logs, and along the edges of swamps or bogs. Imperiled in our area and only found in Pend Oreille County in northeastern Washington. Also called: creeping snowberry.

Slender false-wintergreen (*G. ovatifolia*) has reddish, hairy (rather than hairless) calyxes and finely serrated, pointy-tipped leaves 1–2 in long. Grows in moist to wet forests, heaths

Alpine false-wintergreen (*G. humifusa*)

Hairy false-wintergreen (*G. hispidula*)

WARNING: *Oil of wintergreen, which is most concentrated in the berries and young leaves, contains methyl salicylate, a compound that can cause accidental poisoning. It should never be taken internally, except in very small amounts. Avoid applying the oil when you are hot, because dangerous amounts could be absorbed through the open pores of your skin. It is known to cause skin reactions and severe (anaphylactic) allergic reactions. People who are allergic to aspirin should not use false-wintergreen or its relatives.*

Alpine false-wintergreen (*G. humifusa*)

and bogs in montane and subalpine sites. Common in the Cascades, Olympics and Siskiyous.

Slender false-wintergreen (*G. ovatifolia*)

Slender false-wintergreen (*G. ovatifolia*)

135

Salal *Gaultheria shallon*

Also called: Oregon wintergreen

Salal (*G. shallon*)

These dark, juicy berries grow in many places on the Pacific coast and were traditionally the most plentiful and important fruit gathered by Native Americans living within the plant's range. The berries were eaten fresh, dried into cakes (weighing as much as 15 lbs!) for winter or used as an important trade item, and they continue to be relished today. The Quileute dipped whole clusters of ripe fruit in whale or seal oil and plucked the berries off with their teeth. For trading, selling or as food for common people, ripe salal berries were often mixed with currants, elderberries or unripe salal berries. Cakes of pure salal berries were reserved for immediate family members or chiefs at feasts. In many Coast Salish languages, the month of August is named for the ripening of salal berries.

In recent times, salal berries have been prepared as jams or preserves. The ripe berries from prime bushes are hard to beat for flavor and juiciness. They can be used in any recipes that traditionally call for blueberries, for example, in syrups, pancakes, muffins, cookies and fruitcakes. To make a refreshing drink, crush the berries and cook them, adding an equal measure of water. Strain using a fine cloth (salal seeds are quite small), add a bit of sugar and/or lemon juice to enhance the flavor, if desired, and chill the resulting mixture.

The fruit, which quickly stains your fingers while picking, also makes a good purple dye. The glossy, green leaves are widely harvested for export and sold to florists worldwide for use in floral arrangements. If you are gathering these fruits with children, pick a single berry off its stem and gently squeeze the stem end between your thumb and index finger. If your chosen berry is a ripe and juicy one, this pressure will cause the blossom end to open out into a flower-shaped fruit. It's fun to make a "flower" out of a berry—and it's tasty to eat!

EDIBILITY: highly edible

FRUIT: Purplish black, berry-like capsules to ³/₈ in across.

SEASON: Flowers March to June. Fruit ripens August to September.

DESCRIPTION: Erect to partially creeping, freely branching, evergreen shrub to 10 ft tall, often forming thickets. Leaves broadly oval, dark green, glossy, 1½–5 in long, ½–3 in wide, finely serrated, dark green on top, lighter beneath. Leaf stalks, flower stems, bracts and young branches reddish, hairy and sometimes sticky. Flowers white to pinkish, urn-shaped, 5-lobed, ³/₈ in long, in clusters of 5–15. Often grows on rotting logs and stumps. An abundant shrub over much of the Pacific coast, growing in dry to wet forests, bogs and openings to montane elevations in the Cascades and westward; much less common east of the Cascades; also found in the Blue Mountains.

Bearberries & Manzanitas *Arctostaphylos* spp.

Common bearberry (*A. uva-ursi*)

Bearberries are rather mealy and tasteless, but they are often abundant and remain on branches all year, so they can be an important survival food. Many Native Americans traditionally ate them. To reduce the dryness, bearberries were often cooked with salmon oil, bear fat or fish eggs, or were added to soups or stews. Boiled bearberries were sometimes preserved in oil and served whipped with snow during winter, or they were sweetened with syrup or sugar and served with cream, reportedly making a tasty dessert. They can also be used in jams, jellies, cobblers and pies, or dried, ground and cooked into a mush. Apparently, if the berries are fried in grease over a slow fire, they eventually pop, rather like popcorn. Scalded, mashed berries, soaked in water for an hour or so, produce a spicy, cider-like drink, which can be sweetened and fermented to make wine.

Manzanita berries are very similar to bearberries. They are said to be best just before they are fully ripe, and these berries were historically eaten fresh, used to make cider and smoked as a pipe herb. Hikers sometimes chew the berries and leaves to stimulate saliva flow and relieve thirst. Manzanitas are a very challenging group to identify if you live in an area such as southwestern Oregon, which has several species. Pay close attention to the presence or absence of a burl, a gnarled structure at the base of the tree with buds that can resprout if the rest of the tree is damaged by fire. Also note the bark characteristics on older twigs and hair patterning on the younger twigs, as well as leaf shape and indumenta (the presence of hairs or scales).

Although bearberry diversity is higher north of our region (there are 3 species in British Columbia), manzanita diversity is higher south of our region, with a whopping 59 species and 9 named hybrids in California!

EDIBILITY: edible but not palatable

FRUIT: Small drupes (berries), $^3/_{16}$–$^3/_8$ in across, bright red to purplish black.

SEASON: Flowers May to July. Fruit ripens August to September.

DESCRIPTION: Evergreen or deciduous shrubs with clusters of nodding, white or pinkish, urn-shaped flowers and juicy to mealy, berry-like drupes containing 5 small nutlets. The genus *Arctostaphylos* contains 2 main groups of species: bearberries, which are low, trailing to tufted shrubs found most abundantly in alpine regions, and manzanitas, which are taller, erect or spreading shrubs.

Common bearberry (*A. uva-ursi*) is a trailing, evergreen shrub to 6 in tall. Leaves leathery, evergreen, spoon-shaped, $^3/_8$–1 in long. Flowers $^1/_4$ in long, appearing from May to June. Fruits bright red, mealy, $^3/_{16}$–$^3/_8$ in across, in late summer. Grows in well-drained, often gravelly or sandy soils in open woods and on rocky, exposed sites at all elevations throughout our region. Also called: kinnikinnick.

Eastwood's manzanita (*A. glandulosa*) is a mound-forming shrub 3–10 ft tall, growing from a basal burl. Twigs with long, clear to pink, sometimes glandular hairs. Leaves 1–2 in long, half as wide, variously hairy or not, serrated or not. Less common than hoary manzanita but within the same range (southwestern Oregon). Occasional hybrids (*A. × parvifolia*) with pinemat manzanita can be found in Josephine and Jackson Counties in Oregon.

Common bearberry (*A. uva-ursi*)

139

Common bearberry (*A. uva-ursi*)

Gasquet manzanita (*A. hispidula*) either grows upright or as a shrub, 3–10 ft tall, not burled. Twigs covered with fine, glandular hairs. Leaves ⅜–1 in long, half as wide, with smooth margins, rough surfaces and fine, glandular hairs. Also found in southwestern Oregon.

Greenleaf manzanita (*A. patula*) is a spreading shrub that grows 3–6 ft tall. Bark smooth, reddish brown on older branches. Burl usually absent. Leaves bright yellowish green, egg-shaped, 1–2 in long, smooth. Fruits brownish. Found in the mountains at low elevations. Restricted to Chelan and Klickitat Counties in Washington but found throughout the Cascades and Siskiyous in Oregon.

Greenleaf manzanita (*A. patula*)

Hoary manzanita (*A. canescens*)

Hairy manzanita (*A. columbiana*) is a much taller shrub, 3–10 ft high. Leaves 1–2 in long, oval, evergreen. Fruits red. Grows in open, coniferous forests and openings in western Washington. Can hybridize with common bearberry to form *A.* × *media*, which is found on the eastern side of the Olympic Peninsula and more sporadically along the Oregon coast and in the Willamette Valley.

Hoary manzanita (*A. canescens*) grows to 10 ft tall and is not burled. Small branches covered with short, soft hairs. Leaves 1–2 in long, half as wide, with smooth margins and hairless surfaces. Flowers white to pink, in hanging clusters. Fruits $^3/_{16}$–$^3/_8$ in wide, slightly hairy to smooth with separate seeds (stones). Found in the Siskiyous and southwestern Oregon in rocky, open areas.

Hairy manzanita (*A. columbiana*)

141

Pinemat manzanita (*A. nevadensis*)

Pinemat manzanita (*A. nevadensis*) is a spreading, mat-forming shrub with horizontal stems. Leaves ½–1 in long. Can be distinguished from bearberry by the fruit, which is reddish with splotches of black or brown (vs. bright red without splotches in bearberry). Grows at middle elevations in the Cascades, Siskiyous and the mountains of eastern Oregon.

Sticky whiteleaf manzanita (*A. viscida*) grows upright to 10 ft tall, burl absent. Twigs smooth, sparsely hairy or with dense, glandular hairs. Leaves dull whitish, 1–2 in long, nearly as wide, with smooth or hairy margins. Branches of flower clusters are sticky (viscid). Also found in southwestern Oregon but not coastal.

Waldo manzanita (*A.* × *cinerea*) is a hybrid of hoary manzanita and sticky whiteleaf manzanita with features intermediate between the 2 species. Range in our area is restricted to southwestern Oregon.

Sticky whiteleaf manzanita (*A. viscida*)

142

Gasquet manzanita (*A. hispidula*)

Eastwood's manzanita (*A. glandulosa*)

Pinemat manzanita (*A. nevadensis*)

Black Crowberry   *Empetrum nigrum*

Also called: moss berry, curlew berry

Black crowberry (*Empetrum nigrum*)

Although they are one of the most abundant edible wild fruits found in northern regions and were a vital addition to the diet of northern Native Americans, crowberries are restricted in our area to exposed, rocky bluffs and the limited number of coastal and inland peat bogs. Probably as a result of the abundance of other, tastier berries, there is little record of crowberry use by the Native Americans in our area.

Because crowberries are almost devoid of natural acids, they can taste a little bland and were often mixed with blueberries and lard or oil and, in more modern times, with sugar and

lemon. Their taste does seem to vary greatly with habitat—the flavor of the berries has been described as ranging from bland to delicious to somewhat like turpentine. The taste improves after freezing or cooking, however, and their sweetness peaks after a frost.

Crowberries are high in vitamin C and have about twice that of blueberries. They are also rich in antioxidant anthocyanins, the pigment that gives them their black color. Their high water content was a blessing to hunters seeking to quench their thirst in the waterless high country. The berries have a firm, impermeable skin and are not prone to becoming soggy, so they

are ideal for making muffins, pancakes, pies, jellies (with added pectin), preserves and the like. For a fine dessert, cook the berries with a little lemon juice and serve them with cream and sugar.

Crowberries are usually collected in fall, but because they often persist on the plant over winter, they can be picked (snow depth permitting) through to spring if wildlife doesn't get them first. These fruits are small, so it can take up to 1 hour to pick 2 cups of berries! Consuming too many crowberries may cause constipation, so they have historically been prescribed for diarrhea. The berries also make a reasonable black dye.

EDIBILITY: edible

FRUIT: Juicy, black, shiny, berry-like drupes, 1/8–3/8 in across, containing 2–9 large, inedible seeds, sometimes overwintering.

SEASON: Flowers May to August. Fruit ripens July to November.

DESCRIPTION: Evergreen dwarf or low shrub, 2–4 in tall, prostrate and mat-forming, to 1 ft long. Leaves dark to yellowish green to wine-colored, 1/16–1/4 in long, needle-like, alternate but growing so closely together as to appear whorled. Flowers inconspicuous, 1–3, pink, in leaf axils, 3 petals and 3 sepals, the petals 1/8 in long, male and female flowers separate but on the same plant. Grows prolifically in bogs, moist, shady forests, low-lying headlands and dry, acidic, rocky or gravelly soil on slopes, ridges and seashores.

Mulberry *Morus alba*

White mulberry (*M. alba*)

Perhaps because of its sweet, juicy fruit, the circumambulation of mulberry bushes (specifically black mulberry, *M. nigra*) has won its way into nursery rhymes. An American version of the English rhyme "Pop Goes the Weasel" sings out,

> *All around the mulberry bush,*
> *The monkey chased the weasel,*
> *The monkey stopped to pull up*
> *   his sock,*
> *"Pop!" goes the weasel.*

Another English nursery rhyme, "Here We Go Round the Mulberry Bush," focuses more exclusively on the mulberry,

> *Here we go round the mulberry bush,*
> *The mulberry bush,*
> *The mulberry bush,*
> *Here we go round the mulberry bush,*
> *So early in the morning.*

Not only are fresh mulberries worthy of childish praise, but the fruit can also be fermented into a number of alcoholic beverages capable of producing similar spinning sensations among even the less-nimble adult population. White mulberry fruit has been used medicinally by the Chinese to prevent the premature graying of hair and

promote longevity. The fruit is very high in vitamins A, B1, B2 and C, as well as protein, lipids and anthocyanins. Mulberry leaves have important medicinal uses, and leaf decoctions are used to inhibit bacterial infections and treat diabetes. The leaves are important forage for silkworms and livestock, and even silkworm feces are used medicinally by the Chinese.

Because of their delicate nature, mulberries are best eaten fresh or processed immediately. Large quantities can be quickly harvested by shaking the berries onto tarps.

EDIBILITY: edible, tasty

FRUIT: White, fleshy, aggregate berries (similar to blackberries), typically longer than wide, usually less than 1 in long, with black, purple or nearly white flesh and black seeds; sweet and juicy but bland.

SEASON: Flowers in May and June. Fruit ripens throughout mid-July and August.

DESCRIPTION: Small to medium-sized tree 30–50 ft tall. Leaves deciduous, 4–10 in long, serrated margins, variously unlobed or lobed (mitten shape is common). Flowers and fruit borne on slender stalks; male and female flowers are variously on the same or different trees. Introduced from Asia and has escaped cultivation to grow in disturbed areas, especially along rivers and streams. Most commonly found in the Columbia River Gorge and sporadically in eastern Washington and eastern Oregon. Differs from red mulberry (*M. rubra*), which isn't known to grow wild in our area, by having leaves with smooth surfaces (vs. rough in red mulberry) and hairs on the leaf undersides that are limited to major veins or absent altogether (the undersides of red mulberry leaves are completely covered with fine hairs).

Netleaf Hackberry
Celtis laevigata var. *reticulata*

Also called: western hackberry, Douglas hackberry • *C. occidentalis, C. douglasii, C. reticulata*

Netleaf hackberry (*C. laevigata* var. *reticulata*)

Netleaf hackberry fruit was traditionally eaten by Native Americans in the desert Southwest and probably on the Columbia Plateau as well (it has a Sahaptin name). The berries were eaten fresh or ground into a fine pulp (seeds and all) and formed into cakes that were cooked and eaten, or dried for future use. Netleaf hackberry wood was used by homesteaders for rough furniture, fenceposts and firewood. The leaves and branches can be boiled to produce a dark brown or red dye for wool. Allelopathic compounds that leach out of the fallen leaves and twigs prevent other vegetation from growing under netleaf hackberry trees.

There are 60 to 70 species of hackberry globally, mostly in the warm temperate regions of the Northern Hemisphere. Eight species and 4 subspecies are found in the U.S., but 2 of these are introduced. Hackberries are highly edible and, according to Midwest foraging expert Sam Thayer, vastly underappreciated. He writes in his book *Nature's Garden* that their abundance in archaeological sites around the world makes them among the most important food plants to hunter-gatherers. Hackberries may also be the oldest known human plant food; judging from remains found in

China in association with Peking Man, they were eaten 500,000 years ago. The crushed fruit has a natural balance of carbohydrates, oils and proteins. With a stellar nutrient profile and fine flavor, hackberry products could easily be marketed to environmentally conscious foodies wherever they grow, though perhaps they would do best if sold under a more appetizing name.

EDIBILITY: highly edible, sweet, large-seeded

FRUIT: Deep reddish purple to black, berry-like drupes, $1/4$–$3/8$ in wide, with a thin, sweet-tasting rind over a large, hard-shelled seed that has a date-like filling. As a food plant, they are mostly ignored today by people who don't know any better, but are eaten by squirrels and birds. Hackberries should be crushed and ground finely enough that the shell fragments aren't noticeable, or crushed and strained to remove the hard bits.

SEASON: Flowers April and May. Fruit ripens in fall.

DESCRIPTION: Scraggly tree or stunted shrub usually 10–30 ft tall. Bark gray to reddish brown, thick, with a warty, corky-ridged texture. Leaves alternate, 2–4 in long, lance-shaped to oval with unequal bases, serrated or entire margins, net-like veins. Grows on open slopes and rocky bluffs in the Columbia and Snake River watersheds.

149

Elderberries *Sambucus* spp.

Red elderberry (*S. racemosa*)

Raw red elderberries are generally considered inedible and the cooked berries edible (see Warning), but some tribes are said to have eaten large quantities fresh from the bush. Cooking or drying destroys the rank-smelling, toxic compounds, and most elderberries were consumed after steaming or boiling, or were dried for winter use. Raw blue elderberries are far more palatable than raw red elderberries, but they should be frozen, dried or cooked to further improve their flavor and to detoxify them before large quantities are consumed. Sometimes, clusters of blue elderberry fruit were spread on beds of pine needles in late autumn and covered with more needles and eventually an insulating layer of snow. These caches were easily located in the winter months by the bluish pink stain they left in the snow! Only small amounts of the berries were were eaten at a time, though, just enough to get a taste. Sometimes elderberries were steamed with black hair lichen for flavoring. Today, both red and blue species are used in jams, jellies, syrups, preserves, pies and wine. Because these fruits contain no pectin, they are often mixed with tart, pectin-rich fruits such as crab apples.

Elderberries are also used to make teas and to flavor some wines (e.g., Liebfraumilch). A delicious, refreshing fizzy drink called elderflower pressé or cordial can be made from the flowers. Red elderberry juice was sometimes used to marinate salmon prior to baking. The flowers can be used to make tea or wine, and in some areas, flower clusters were popular dipped in batter and fried as fritters or stripped from their relatively bitter stalks and mixed into pancake batter.

Elderberries are rich in vitamins A and C, calcium, potassium and iron. They have also been shown to contain antiviral compounds that could be useful in treating influenza. The berries can be used to produce a brilliant crimson or violet dye.

Red elderberry (*S. racemosa*)

Blue elderberry (*S. cerulea*)

Elderberry wine, elderberries soaked in buttermilk and elderflower water have all been used in cosmetic washes and skin creams. The genus name *Sambucus* is derived from *sambuke*, the name of a Greek musical instrument, in reference to the hollow, pithy stems of this plant, which have been used in many different cultures to make musical instruments.

EDIBILITY: edible with caution, considered toxic

FRUIT: Juicy, berry-like drupes, ¼ in across, in dense, showy clusters.

SEASON: Blooms April to July. Fruit ripens July to September.

DESCRIPTION: Unpleasant-smelling, deciduous shrubs 5–20 ft tall, with pithy, opposite branches often sprouting from the base. Leaves compound, pinnately divided into 5–9 sharply toothed leaflets 2–6 in long. Flowers white, ¼ in wide, in crowded, branched clusters.

Blue elderberry (*S. cerulea*)

Blue elderberry (*S. cerulea*) has flat-topped flower clusters and dull blue fruits with a whitish bloom. Bark on new growth is reddish orange. Leaves with multiple leaflets, usually 9. Grows in gravelly, dry soils along streambanks, field edges and in woodlands. Much more common east of the Cascades but occasionally found on the western side. Also called: *S. mexicana, S. nigra* ssp. *cerulea.*

Red elderberry (*S. racemosa*) has pyramid-shaped flower clusters and shiny fruits. We have 2 common varieties: black elderberry (var.

Blue elderberry (*S. cerulea*)

melanocarpa) with purplish black fruit in flat-topped clusters, grows predominantly east of the Cascade crest in the mountains; and red elderberry (var. *pubens*), a coastal species with red fruit in pyramidal clusters. Both varieties grow in open woods and along forest edges and roadsides, as well as on montane and subalpine sites. Also called: *S. melanocarpa, S. pubens*.

Red elderberry (*S. racemosa*)

Black elderberry
(*S. racemosa* var. *melanocarpa*)

WARNING: *All parts of this plant except for the fruit and flowers are considered toxic. The stems, bark, leaves and roots contain poisonous cyanide-producing glycosides (especially when fresh), which cause nausea, vomiting and diarrhea, but the ripe fruits and flowers are edible. The seeds, however, contain toxins that are most concentrated in red-fruited species. Many sources classify red-fruited elderberries as poisonous and black- or blue-fruited species as edible.*

Red elderberry (*S. racemosa*)

Red elderberry (*S. racemosa*)

153

Bush-cranberries & Viburnums *Viburnum* spp.

Highbush cranberry (*V. edule*)

Raw bush-cranberries are high in vitamin C and can be very sour and acidic (much like true cranberries), but many native peoples ate them, chewing the fruit, swallowing the juice and spitting out the tough skins and seeds. These berries were traditionally mixed with grease and stored in birchbark baskets for winter use, trade or a valuable gift. They were also eaten with bear grease or, in an early year, they could be mixed with sweeter berries such as serviceberries. Some tribes ate the boiled berries mixed with oil, and occasionally this mixture was whipped with fresh snow to make a frothy dessert.

Bush-cranberries are an excellent winter survival food because they remain on the branches all winter and are high enough above the ground that the snow doesn't cover them. The berries are best picked in autumn, after they have been softened and sweetened by a frost. Some people compare their fragrance to that of

Highbush cranberry (*V. edule*)

Highbush cranberry (*V. edule*)

dirty socks, but the flavor is good (perhaps a Stilton of the berry world?). The addition of lemon or orange peel to the fruit, however, is said to eliminate this odor.

Today, bush-cranberries are usually boiled, strained to remove the seeds and skins, and used in jams and jellies. Although these preserves usually require additional pectin, especially after the berries have been frozen, there are reports that imperfectly ripe berries (not yet red) jell without added pectin. Bush-cranberry juice can be used to make a refreshing cold drink or fermented to make wine, and the fresh or dried berries can be steeped in hot water to make tea. Unfortunately, the large stones and tough skins limit their use in muffins, pancakes and pies. The berries produce a lovely reddish pink

European bush-cranberry (*V. opulus* var. *opulus*)

American bush-cranberry (*V. opulus* var. *americanum*)

but also a showy fall foliar display and important winter wildlife food—if the humans don't get there first! If possible, taste the berries from nursery stock before purchasing because European bush-cranberry (*V. opulus* var. *opulus*), which has horrible-tasting fruit, is often mistakenly sold as our native American bush-cranberry (*V. o.* var. *americana*) or even the better-tasting highbush cranberry (*V. edule*).

EDIBILITY: highbush cranberry and American bush-cranberry are edible, especially after cooking or freezing; use other species with caution as they are possibly toxic

FRUIT: Juicy, strong-smelling, red to orange, berry-like drupes, ½ in long, with 1 flat stone.

SEASON: Flowers April to July. Fruit ripens September to October.

dye, and the acidic juice can be used as a mordant (a chemical that sets dyes and makes the color permanent).

American bush-cranberry makes a wonderful garden ornamental that is drought tolerant and provides not only pretty, scented spring flowers,

European bush-cranberry (*V. opulus* var. *opulus*)

WARNING: *Some sources classify raw bush-cranberries as poisonous, whereas others report that they were commonly eaten raw by native peoples. Ingesting a few berries may be harmless, but eating large quantities can cause vomiting and cramps, especially if the fruit is not fully ripe, so it is probably best to cook the berries before eating. Despite the common name "cranberry," these species are not botanically related to the sour, red berries we traditionally enjoy with a Thanksgiving feast.*

Leatherleaf viburnum (*V. rhytidophyllum*)

DESCRIPTION: Deciduous shrubs 1–15 ft tall. Leaves opposite, 1–6 in long, turning a showy red in fall. Flowers white, small, 5-petaled, forming flat-topped clusters.

American bush-cranberry (*V. opulus* var. *americanum*) is a large shrub 3–15 feet tall, with a wide-spreading habit. Leaves opposite, maple-like, with 3 relatively deeply cut lobes. Flower clusters a showy outer ring of large (½–1 in wide), white, sterile flowers surrounding tiny, petal-less blooms. Grows in moist soils, hedges, scrub areas, plains and woodlands. Found planted or escaped from

Highbush cranberry (*V. edule*), left, and European bush-cranberry (*V. opulus* var. *opulus*), right

European bush-cranberry (*V. opulus* var. *opulus*)

cultivation in eastern Puget Sound, the Columbia River Gorge and eastern Washington, as well as the Willamette Valley in Oregon. Note that the name "American bush-cranberry" is sometimes attributed to *V. edule*. Also called: highbush cranberry, American cranberrybush • *V. trilobum*.

European bush-cranberry (*V. opulus* var. *opulus*) looks nearly identical to American bush-cranberry but has smaller, wider leaves with more teeth. European bush-cranberry occupies a similar range, but has skunky-tasting fruit that can only be eaten after extensive cooking and sweetening.

Highbush cranberry (*V. edule*) is a scraggly-looking shrub 1–10 ft tall.

Bark smooth, gray with a reddish tinge. Leaves opposite, 1–4 in wide, sharply toothed, often with 3 shallow lobes near the leaf tip, hairy underneath, both surfaces with scattered glands. Petioles (leaf stalks) usually have a pair of glandular projections near the intersection with the leaf. Flowers small, $3/16-1/4$ in across, in relatively inconspicuous clusters beneath leaf pairs; stamens do not extend beyond the flowers. Distinctive, musky smell may announce its presence before it is actually seen. Grows in shady foothills, damp woods, streambank thickets, swamps and some montane and subalpine sites. Found on both sides of the Cascades in Washington and northern Oregon. Also called: mooseberry, squashberry, bush-cranberry.

Japanese snowball (*V. plicatum*), similar to oval-leaved viburnum, has unlobed, elliptic leaves 2–4 in long and 1–3 in wide. Fertile flowers form a "snowball-like" cluster in the center of a ring of large, infertile flowers. Fruits blue-black drupes of unknown edibility. Introduced from Japan, it has escaped cultivation in the Willamette Valley.

Leatherleaf viburnum (*V. rhytidophyllum*) is similar to oval-leaved viburnum but is a tall shrub 10–15 ft high with long, unlobed, downy leaves. It has (rarely) escaped cultivation in the Willamette Valley.

Oval-leaved viburnum (*V. ellipticum*) is an upright shrub 3–10 ft tall. Leaves opposite, 1–3 in long, coarsely blunt-toothed, with short, stiff hairs and 3 or 5 major veins. Petioles (leaf stalks) with long hairs and often a linear stipule (leaf-like appendage),

Japanese snowball (*V. plicatum*)

$^1/_8$–$^3/_8$ in long, where the stalks connect to the stem. Flowers white, $^1/_4$–$^3/_8$ in wide, in clusters 1–2 inches wide at branch tips. Fruits red, 1-seeded drupes. Grows in floodplains and open forests west of the Cascades in southwestern Washington and in western Oregon.

Oval-leaved viburnum (*V. ellipticum*)

Honeysuckles *Lonicera* spp.

Tatarian honeysuckle (*L. tatarica*)

Honeysuckles are members of the Caprifoliaceae (literally "goat leaf") family. They are best known for the sweet nectar of their flowers, from which birds, bees and even children gleefully sip. The fragrance of honeysuckles fills the air with mystical delight, especially at night. In Shakespeare's *A Midsummer Night's Dream*, European honeysuckle formed a canopy over the sleeping place of Titania, the queen of the fairies. Honeysuckle flowers appeal to the visual sense as well, and our native species are among the prettiest flowers in the woods.

The genus name *Lonicera* honors 16th-century German botanist Adam Lonicer (1528–86).

EDIBILITY: some species edible, at least 1 species mildly toxic (black twinberry, *L. involucrata*, pp. 218–19), others inedible and of unknown toxicity

FRUIT: Many-seeded berries, usually red or orange but blue in one species.

SEASON: Flowers late spring and early summer. Fruit ripens late summer and early fall.

DESCRIPTION: Woody vines and deciduous shrubs with opposite leaves usually less than 2 in long. Flowers often fragrant, tubular with somewhat spreading petals and 5 stamens, arising from leaf axils or in terminal clusters.

Chaparral honeysuckle (*L. interrupta*) is a trailing to climbing shrub with a stout, woody trunk. Leaves opposite, 1 in long, oval to round, the terminal 1–3 pairs fused around the stem.

Flowers 2-lipped, cream to yellow, ⅜ in long. Fruit red, ⅜ in across. Edibility of berries unknown but flowers have sweet nectar. Found in chaparral habitat. Limited in our area to south-western Oregon around Jackson County.

Etruscan honeysuckle (*L. etrusca*) is a trailing or climbing, hollow-stemmed vine 10–15 ft tall/long. Leaves opposite, oval, 2–5 in long, 1–2 in wide, soft-haired, with very short stalks (nearly stalkless). Flowers pinkish white, in dense terminal clusters above a pair of fused leaves. Berries red, ½ in wide. Introduced from Europe to our area, where it has established itself along the Oregon coast and sporadically on the Washington coast.

European honeysuckle (*L. periclyme-num*) is a strongly climbing deciduous vine climbing to 30 ft tall/long. Flowers sweet-smelling, creamy white to yellow. Native to Europe and planted widely in our area for its beauty, this species has escaped from cultivation in western Washington and western Oregon. Also called: woodbine.

Orange honeysuckle (*L. ciliosa*)

Orange honeysuckle (*L. ciliosa*) is a deciduous, hollow-stemmed, woody vine, climbing to 20 ft tall/long. Leaves opposite, egg-shaped, 2–4 in long, 1–2 in wide, nearly stalkless, the terminal 1–2 pairs fused together, hairless except for a few hairs along leaf margins. Flowers orange, tubular, in dense terminal clusters. Berries red, ⅜ in wide. Fruit not known to be edible, but flowers produce sweet, harmless nectar. Found in dry forests from low to middle elevations on both

European honeysuckle (*L. periclymenum*)

Utah honeysuckle (*L. utahensis*)

sides of the Cascades and on the east slope of the Olympics and Coast Range. Widely used as a medicine by Native Americans.

Pink honeysuckle (*L. hispidula*) is a vine that can either take on a shrubby form or climb to 20 ft tall. Stem hollow, blue-green when young. Leaves opposite, 2–3 inches long, robust, the terminal pair fused together. Flowers whitish pink or yellowish pink, in vertically elongated clusters on well-developed flower stalks arising both terminally and in leaf axils. Berries red, ½ in wide.

Pink honeysuckle (*L. hispidula*)

Not known to be edible to humans but eaten by birds. Found in open woods at low elevations west of the Cascades. Hollow stems used as smoking pipes by Native Americans.

Privet honeysuckle (*L. pileata*) is an evergreen shrub that grows 2–3 ft tall. Leaves opposite, ½–1 in long. Berries ripen to blue or purple. An escaped ornamental.

Purpleflower honeysuckle (*L. conjugialis*) is a deciduous shrub 1½–4½ ft tall. Leaves opposite, on short petioles, 1–3 in long, half as wide, smooth margins, stiff-haired on the underside and sometimes on upper surface as well. Flowers 2-lipped, auburn, on long stalks arising singly from leaf axils. Fruit red to black, ⅜ in wide, in pairs that are sometimes fused together, giving them a bosom-like appearance that has led California botanist Keir Morse to call them "boob-berries." The berries are occasionally eaten by the Klamath in Oregon. Found on either side of the Oregon Cascade crest in high-elevation, open forests and plains, often near water.

Sweetberry honeysuckle (*L. caerulea*) is a deciduous shrub that grows to 7 ft tall. Leaves opposite, oval, 2 in long, 1 in wide, smooth margins, whitish green with a waxy texture. Flowers yellowish white, ½ in long, in pairs near the base of new stem growth; blooms in June and July. Both flowers and young stems long-haired. Fruit blue, to ½ in wide and 1 in long, edible both fresh and cooked into jam, jelly or juice. Found in open woods from low to middle elevations in southeastern Washington, the Oregon Cascades and the Wallowa Mountains. Also called: blue-berried honeysuckle; honeyberry.

Tatarian honeysuckle (*L. tatarica*) is a hollow-stemmed, deciduous shrub growing to 10 ft tall. Leaves opposite, 1–2 in long, oval. Flowers pink to red, in pairs arising from leaf axils. Berries bright orange or red, horrid-tasting but of unknown toxicity. Introduced from Siberia and now a troublesome invasive throughout North America. Fortunately not yet widespread in our region. Grows in disturbed areas.

Purpleflower honeysuckle (*L. conjugialis*)

Utah honeysuckle (*L. utahensis*) is a deciduous shrub 3–6 ft tall. Leaves opposite, 1–3 in long, elliptic, smooth above, stiff-haired on the underside. Flowers light yellow to slightly green, in pairs, arising in leaf axils on stalks 2–6 in long. Berries bright red, about ⅜ in wide, edible and eaten by the Colville. Found at middle to high elevations in the Cascade, Olympic, Blue and Wallowa mountain ranges.

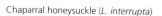

Chaparral honeysuckle (*L. interrupta*)

Sweetberry honeysuckle (*L. caerulea*)

Soapberry *Shepherdia canadensis*

Also called: russet buffaloberry

Soapberry (*S. canadensis*)

Soapberries were an important fruit for Native Americans within the plant's range, either for home use or as a trade item. The berries were eaten fresh or were boiled, formed into cakes and dried over a small fire for future use. Because their juice is rich in saponin, soapberries become foamy when beaten. The ripe fruit was mixed about 4:1 with water and whipped like egg whites to make a foamy dessert called "Indian ice cream." The resulting foam is truly unexpected and remarkable, with a beautiful white to pale pink color and a smooth, shiny consistency similar to that of the best whipped meringue! Traditionally, this dessert was beaten by hand or with a special stick with grass or strands of bark tied to one end, but these tools were eventually replaced by eggbeaters and mixers. Like egg whites, soapberries will not foam in plastic or greasy containers. The incredibly thick foam is

rather bitter, so it was usually sweetened with sugar or with other berries. Soapberries can also be added to stews or cooked to make syrup, jelly, jam or a sauce for savory meats. Canned soapberry juice mixed with sugar and water makes a refreshing "lemonade."

Although they are bitter, soapberries are often abundant and can be used in moderation as an emergency food (see Warning). The berries were traditionally collected by beating the branches over a canvas or hide, and then rolling the fruit down a wooden board into

Soapberry (*S. canadensis*)

a container to separate leaves and other debris.

Soapberries are rich in vitamin C and iron. They have been used to treat flu and indigestion, and have been made into a medicinal tea for relieving constipation. Canned soapberry juice, mixed with sugar and water, was used to treat acne, boils, digestive problems and gallstones. Soapberry bark tea was a favorite solution for eye troubles. These berries can also be crushed or boiled to use as a liquid soap.

EDIBILITY: edible but bitter

FRUIT: Juicy, bright red, oval berries with a fine, silvery scale, on very short stalks in leaf axils on female plants.

SEASON: Flowers April. Fruit ripens July to September.

DESCRIPTION: Deciduous shrub, open-formed, to 6 ft tall. Young twigs covered in a brown or rusty scale. Older twigs and branches brownish red with orange flecks, sometimes fissured. Leaves opposite, somewhat thick, elliptic, smooth-edged, tip rounded, upper surface green with short, silvery scales, rusty underneath when young. Flowers yellowish to greenish, male and female flowers on separate plants, single or in small clusters. Grows in open woods, mixed forests and on streambanks. Prefers moist habitats but will tolerate some drought. Found in northern Washington and scattered in eastern Oregon.

Silver buffaloberry (*S. argentea*) is also 1–6 ft tall. Leaves 1–2 in long, oval with rounded tips, silver on both sides, covered with dense layer of fine, silvery hairs. Fruit red. Restricted in our area to southeastern Oregon

WARNING: *This species contains saponin, a bitter, soapy substance that can irritate the stomach and cause diarrhea, vomiting and cramps if consumed in large amounts.*

in Harney and Malheur Counties, where it grows close to water.

Silver buffaloberry (*S. argentea*)

Indian Ice Cream

Makes approximately 6 cups

Even with sugar this treat will have a slightly bitter taste, but many people quickly grow to like it.

1 cup soapberries • 1 cup water
4 Tbsp granulated white sugar

Put berries and water into a wide-topped ceramic or glass mixing bowl. *Do not use a plastic bowl or utensils, and make sure that nothing is greasy, or the berries will not whip properly.* Whip the mixture with an electric mixer or hand whisk until it reaches the consistency of beaten egg whites. Gradually add the sugar to the pink foam, but not too fast or the foam will "sink." Serve immediately.

Silverberry
Elaeagnus commutata

Also called: wolf willow

Silverberry (*E. commutata*)

The berries of this species are very dry and astringent, but some northern tribes gathered them for food. Most groups considered the mealy berries famine food and did not eat them regularly, but when they did, the berries were consumed either raw or cooked in soup. They were also cooked with blood, mixed with lard and eaten raw, fried in moose fat or frozen. Despite not being very palatable raw, silverberries reportedly make good jams and jellies, and the fruit is apparently much sweeter after exposure to freezing temperatures. Some tribes used the nutlets inside the berries as decorative beads. The berries were boiled to remove the flesh, and while the seeds were still soft, a hole was made through each. They were then threaded, dried, oiled and polished.

The flowers can be detected from several feet away by their sweet, heavy perfume. Some people enjoy this fragrance, but others find it overwhelming and nauseating. If green silverberry wood is burned in a fire, it gives off a strong smell of human excrement! Some practical jokers enjoy sneaking branches into the fire and watching the reactions of fellow campers.

Much better tasting is the introduced autumn olive. Although it currently has a small distribution in Washington and Oregon, it is an aggressive invasive throughout much of the rest of eastern

North America. When fully ripe, the red berries are soft, sweet and delicious, with a flavor reminiscent of raspberries and tomatoes.

EDIBILITY: marginal (Russian olive) to excellent (autumn olive)

FRUIT: Silvery white or red, egg-shaped berries about 1/4–1/2 in wide, with a single, large nutlet.

SEASON: Flowers June to July. Fruit ripens late August to September.

DESCRIPTION: Thicket-forming, rhizomatous shrub 3–20 ft tall. Leaves alternate, 1–5 in long, lance-shaped, deciduous, silvery, covered in dense, tiny, star-shaped hairs (appearing silvery). Flowers strongly sweet-scented, 1/4–5/8 inch long, yellow inside, silvery outside, borne in 2s or 3s in leaf axils. Grows on well-drained, often calcareous slopes, gravel bars and along forest edges at low to montane elevations.

Autumn olive (*E. umbellata*) is a spreading, deciduous shrub that grows 12–20 ft tall. Young stems and leaves covered with brown and silvery hairs. Leaves oval to lance-shaped, 2–5 in long, green. Flowers tubular, 4-lobed, cream-colored, arising from leaf joints. Fruits round, 1/4–3/8 in wide, red, excellent-tasting fresh or dried. A problematic roadside invasive in much of North America, but limited in our area to eastern Puget Sound, the Willamette Valley and the middle to lower reaches of the Columbia River.

Russian olive (*E. angustifolia*) is a spreading tree 10–15 ft tall. Bark brown when young, becoming gray with age, covered with thorns 1–2 in

Russian olive (*E. angustifolia*)

long. Leaves alternate, 1–3 in long, narrowly lance-shaped, covered with small, silvery scales. Flowers fragrant, arising from leaf axils, yellow, solitary or in small clusters. Fruits yellow to greenish gray, olive-shaped, 1/2 in wide, edible, reported to be dry and mealy but sweet. Introduced and historically planted as a windbreak, but now invasive. Grows along streamsides east of the Cascades.

Autumn olive (*E. umbellata*)

Silktassels *Garrya* spp.

Fremont's silktassel (*G. fremontii*)

Silktassels are a hardy group of shrubs that thrive in dry, open environments. All 8 species native to North America are found in the southwestern United States (6 are found in California!) and 3 occur in our area. They are becoming increasingly popular in native landscaping for their early blooming chains of bell-shaped flowers and evergreen foliage but require well-drained soil. The wood is very hard and close-grained and was used by Native Americans for prying shellfish off rocks. Silktassel leaves are extremely bitter and can be used as a febrifuge (fever reducer) and a quinine substitute. The unripe berries produce a gray to black dye but are not edible.

EDIBILITY: inedible

FRUIT: Dry-skinned berries, $1/4$–$3/8$ in wide, fleshy inside, green when young, maturing to purple or black, variously hairy or not.

SEASON: Flowers January through May. Fruit ripens May through July.

DESCRIPTION: Opposite-leaved, evergreen shrubs 3–10 ft tall. Male and female flowers borne on different shrubs in grey-green catkins 1–8 in long. Fruits are round, dry berries containing 2 seeds.

Dwarf silktassel (*G. buxifolia*) is similar to wavyleaf silktassel, growing 3–10 ft tall, but with leaves that are ½–2½ in long with hairy undersides and fruit that is hairless or only slightly hairy at the tip. Found only in the Klamath Mountains in southwestern Oregon.

Fremont's silktassel (*G. fremontii*) is an evergreen shrub that grows 3–10 ft tall. Leaves opposite, elliptic to ovate, 2–3 in long, underside pale yellow-green, with hairless to sparsely haired petioles ½ in long. Plants dioecious (male and female flowers on separate bushes), flowers in racemes 2–4 in long, hanging from leaf axils. Fruits are round, purple berries, ¼ in wide, hairless or only sparsely haired at the tip. Grows in woodlands and chaparral at low to middle elevations along the Columbia River in Washington and Oregon, south through Oregon on the western side of the Cascades and throughout the Klamath Mountains in southwestern Oregon. Also called: bearbrush, California feverbush.

Wavyleaf silktassel (*G. elliptica*) is similar to Fremont's silktassel, growing 3–10 ft tall. Leaves 2–3 in long, densely hairy on the underside, margins wavy and downward-curled. Male flower racemes much longer than female, reaching 12 in long. Fruits round,

purplish black berries, ⅜ in wide, covered with a thick coat of hairs. Found within 20 miles of the ocean along the Oregon coast.

Dwarf silktassel (*G. buxifolia*)

Wayleaf silktassel (*G. elliptica*)

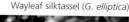

169

Oregon Myrtle   *Umbellularia californica*

Also called: California bay laurel, California bay, California laurel (but not bay laurel)

Oregon myrtle (*Umbellularia californica*)

Oregon myrtle has a long history of use among Native Americans. Both the oily flesh and the dry kernel of the fruit are edible. The fruit, also called "California bay nut" has avocado-like flesh that can be eaten raw when ripe. However, care must be taken to collect it at the right time because immature fruit is filled with intensely flavored volatile oils, and overripe fruit is extremely soft and easily damaged. Traditionally, the upper ⅔ of each fruit was discarded and only the lower ⅓ was eaten because of the strong taste of the upper portion. The kernel must be parched before it can be eaten. Kernels were traditionally eaten in small amounts as a condiment, either whole or pounded into an oily mass that is said to have a coffee-like flavor, though the nuts were not used to make a beverage.

Volatile oils permeate all parts of this plant, and the bark was traditionally used to make a drink. When crushed, the leaves release a strong aroma that can cause headaches, and if brushed on the skin or tongue, have an acrid, camphor-like quality. Oregon myrtle leaves are used today in cooking much like the Mediterranean bay leaf, but they have a much spicier flavor and should be used in moderation. Early settlers and Native Americans used the leaves to drive away fleas by placing the leaves under mattresses or scattering them around infested areas.

EDIBILITY: fruits and seeds edible; leaves can be used as a spice

FRUIT: Round, berry-like drupes, olive-like, 1 in long and slightly narrower, with thin, leathery, green skin spotted with yellow and maturing to purple; oily flesh covers a hard, thin-walled pit.

SEASON: Flowers March to April. Fruit ripens October to November.

DESCRIPTION: Evergreen tree usually less than 100 ft tall with a trunk less than 30 in thick. Leaves lance-shaped, 1–5 in long and ⅓ as wide, with smooth margins. Flowers small, yellowish green, in terminal, umbrella-shaped clusters. Found in canyons and damp areas in redwood and ponderosa pine forests, as well oak woodlands in southwestern Oregon and sporadically northward in the Willamette Valley.

California Wild Grape — *Vitis californica*

California wild grape (*V. californica*)

Indigenous grapes are an important traditional food for Native Americans. There are 15 species (and just about as many varieties and hybrids) native to North America, and all of them are used wherever they are found. Unfortunately, our area lacks both diversity and abundance, and we have 2 species with only marginal distribution. Although very sour, these grapes can be sweetened to make exceptional juice, jelly or wine.

Grape vines are an important basket-weaving material, and the roots are used in viticulture as grafting stalk for many cultivated grape varieties.

EDIBLITY: sour and seedy but edible; best if processed into juice or jelly

FRUIT: Round, purple grapes with juicy pulp and easily separated skin, growing in small clusters along the vines.

SEASON: Flowers late spring and early summer. Fruit ripens in late summer and persists through fall.

DESCRIPTION: Deciduous, woody vine reaching 30 ft long, with peeling bark. Leaves alternate, unlobed or with up to several deep lobes, heart-shaped base, margins wavy to slightly saw-toothed, underside covered with felt-like hairs. Tendrils opposite leaves. Grows along streambanks in south-western Oregon.

Riverbank grape (*V. riparia*) is the most widespread grape in North America but is found only rarely in our area, in the San Juan Islands and the Willamette Valley. Leaves coarsely toothed, 2–10 in long, 2–8 in wide,

WARNING: *Riverbank grapes are high in tartrate, which can cause a burning sensation on the hands and in the mouth. Tartrate is easily removed by letting riverbank grape juice settle for 2 days and carefully decanting the juice off the tartrate sludge that settles on the bottom.*

occasionally with sparsely haired veins on the underside. Grapes dark purple when ripe, $\frac{1}{3}$ in wide, growing in clusters just like their domesticated cousins.

California wild grape (*V. californica*)

Riverbank grape (*V. riparia*)

Riverbank grape (*V. riparia*)

173

One-flowered clintonia (*C. uniflora*)

One-flowered clintonia (*C. uniflora*)

The berries of this species, though very pretty and unusual to look at, are dry, tasteless and mildly toxic so are not recommended for eating. The Cowlitz traditionally mashed the berries to make a wash for sore eyes and cuts. This plant, which spreads through a network of underground rhizomes, matures to form a pretty combination of light green leaves with delicate flowers and metallic blue berries. It is well worth growing for its ornamental value, particularly when planted with other low-growing natives such as bunchberry (white flowers and bright red berry clusters) and trillium (striking white to pink blooms). Birds such as blue grouse relish the berries.

EDIBILITY: edible with caution (mildly toxic)

174

FRUIT: Berries single (rarely double), round to oblong, shiny, bright metallic blue, ¼–½ in across, growing atop a single stem.

SEASON: Flowers May to June. Fruit ripens July to August.

DESCRIPTION: Spreading perennial herb to 20 in tall, arising from rhizomes, often forming colonies. Leaves basal, 2–3 per plant, 1–2 in wide, to 12 in long, shiny, tapered at both ends. Flowers white, 6-petaled, 1 (rarely 2) on a slender, erect stem 6–16 inches tall, usually hairy at the top. Found in shaded, moist to mesic forests and open woods.

Andrew's clintonia (*C. andrewsiana*) is a red-flowered California relative limited in our area to Curry County in southwestern Oregon. The fruits are blue, ⅜ in wide and borne singly or in terminal and lateral clusters of 2–10 along the sparsely leaved inflorescence. Farther south, the fruit was considered poisonous by the Pomo.

Andrew's clintonia (*C. andrewsiana*)

Andrew's clintonia (*C. andrewsiana*)

175

Twisted-stalks   *Streptopus* spp.

Rosy twisted-stalk (*S. lanceolatus*)

These perennials are called "twisted-stalks" because of the kinks (sometimes right-angled, sometimes just a sharp curve) in the main stem and flower stalks. Most Native Americans regarded twisted-stalks as poisonous and used these plants mainly for medicine, but some tribes ate the young shoots and/or brightly colored berries either raw or cooked in soups and stews. The berries are juicy and moderately sweet-tasting but are mildly toxic so should only be eaten in small quantities. Indeed, eating more than a few reportedly causes diarrhea, and it is best to consider these berries inedible.

Twisted-stalks were highly regarded for their general restorative qualities and were taken as a tonic or to treat general sickness. The whole plant was taken by some Native Americans to treat coughs, loss of appetite, stomachaches, spitting up blood, kidney trouble and gonorrhea. The blossoms were ingested to induce sweating. The plant was sometimes tied to, and used to scent, the body, clothes or hair.

Indigenous names for the berries included "owl berries," "witch berries," "black bear berries" and "frog berries." Snakes, deer and wolves were also believed to eat the berries.

Clasping twisted-stalk (*S. amplexifolius*)

Twisted-stalks differ from the closely related fairybells (*Prosartes* spp.) in that the flowers are attached to the stem in the leaf axils instead of to the stem tips. The characteristic, branched stem (sometimes zigzagging) is what separates clasping twisted-stalk from the other twisted-stalks.

EDIBILITY: edible with caution (mildly toxic)

FRUIT: Red-orange or yellowish, egg-shaped, somewhat translucent berries, hanging from leaf axils; seeds small, whitish, somewhat visible.

SEASON: Flowers late June to early August. Fruit ripens August to September.

DESCRIPTION: Slender, herbaceous perennial 16–40 in tall or more, from thick, short rhizomes. Leaves alternate, elliptic or oval, smooth-edged, markedly parallel-veined. Flowers small, white, bell-shaped, 1/3–1/2 in long, 6 backward-curved petals, hanging on lower side of each stalk, 1 per leaf. Found in moist, shaded forests, clearings, meadows, disturbed sites and on streambanks at low to sub-alpine elevations throughout our area.

Rosy twisted-stalk (*S. lanceolatus*)

Clasping twisted-stalk (*S. amplexifolius*) grows 20–40 in tall. Stems branched, smooth, with whitish green prickles near the base, sometimes bent at nodes, giving a zigzag appearance. Leaves clasping at the base. Flowers greenish white. Berries bright red, darkening to purple with age. Found in moist lowland to subalpine forests on both sides of the Cascades.

Rosy twisted-stalk (*S. lanceolatus*) grows to 15 in tall. Stems usually unbranched, curved (not zigzagged). Leaves not clasping at the base. Flowers rose purple or pink with white tips. Berries red. Found in damp woods and along streambanks at middle to high elevations, especially near the Cascade crest. Also called: *S. roseus.*

Clasping twisted-stalk (*S. amplexifolius*)

Rosy twisted-stalk (*S. lanceolatus*)

Clasping twisted-stalk (*S. amplexifolius*)

Small twisted-stalk (*S. streptopoides*) grows 4–8 in tall. Leaves oval to oblong-lance-shaped, smooth, 1–2½ in long, ⅝–¾ in wide. Flowers wine-colored with yellowish green tips, disk-shaped, hanging singly from leaf axils, 1–5 per stem. Berries orange to red, round, ¼ in across. Inhabits damp, dense, coniferous forests at low to middle elevations. Found in the North Cascades and Olympic Mountains in Washington and near Mount Hood in Oregon.

WARNING: *Collecting the young shoots of twisted-stalk for consumption is not recommended unless you are absolutely sure of plant identification!*

Clasping twisted-stalk (*S. amplexifolius*)

Rosy twisted-stalk (*S. lanceolatus*)

Small twisted-stalk (*S. streptopoides*)

Small twisted-stalk (*S. streptopoides*)

False Lily-of-the-valley *Maianthemum dilatatum*

Also called: two-leaved Solomon's-seal

False lily-of-the-valley (*M. dilatatum*)

False lily-of-the-valley berries are considered edible but are bitter-tasting and not very palatable.

Many Native American groups in Washington and Oregon, as well as in neighboring areas, ate false lily-of-the-valley, but it was rarely highly regarded. The berries were usually only eaten casually by children or by hunters and berry pickers while out on trips. Some groups, such as the Haida, used the berries to a great extent. They ate

the berries fresh or picked them when unripe and stored them until they were red and soft. Green berries were sometimes cooked in tall cedar boxes lowered into boiling water for a few minutes, and then the cooked berries were mixed with other fruit before being sun-dried into cakes. Sometimes the berries were scalded and eaten with animal or fish grease or stored this way. These fruits were also used as a medicine for tuberculosis. Caution is advised when eating these berries because ingesting too many can cause severe diarrhea.

The genus name is derived from the Latin word for "May," referring to the flowering time of these plants. The fruit of *Maianthemum* species is a true berry in botanical terms.

EDIBILITY: edible but not palatable

FRUIT: Pea-sized berries, at first hard and green, later developing speckles, and finally becoming soft and red when ripe; borne in clusters at the top of stems.

WILD GARDENING: *This species grows into a delightful, dense carpet of delicate heart-shaped leaves and makes an excellent, low-maintenance understory plant for woodland gardens. The flowers are pretty in spring, and the berries provide a showy late summer and fall display that attracts wildlife such as grouse, which like to eat them.*

SEASON: Flowers May to June. Fruit ripens July to September.

DESCRIPTION: Herbaceous, creeping perennial herb 4–15 in tall, arising from rhizomes and usually forming large colonies. Leaves alternate, usually 2–3, heart-shaped, prominent parallel veins. Flowers small, white, ¼ in wide, 4 petals, in distinct terminal clusters. Found in moist woods and clearings throughout western Washington and the Coast Range in Oregon, with limited distribution in the foothills of the Oregon Cascades.

False Solomon's-seals *Maianthemum* spp.

False Solomon's-seal (*M. racemosum*)

Various Native American groups across the continent ate the ripe berries, young greens and fleshy rhizomes of these species. Some groups on the west coast believed the berries to be the food of snakes and avoided them. When the berries were eaten, it was usually casually by hunters, berry pickers and children. The fruit of both species is traditionally eaten by the Okanagon in the late summer, and false Solomon's-seal berries were also eaten by the Skagit.

The berries of star-flowered false Solomon's-seal are said to be high in vitamin C.

EDIBILITY: edible but not palatable; flavor improves after frost begins to kill the leaves

FRUIT: Small, densely clustered berries, initially green and mottled or striped, ripening to bright red.

SEASON: Flowers May to June. Fruit ripens August to October.

Star-flowered false Solomon's-seal
(*M. stellatum*)

False Solomon's-seal
(*M. racemosum*)

Star-flowered false Solomon's-seal
(*M. stellatum*)

Star-flowered false Solomon's-seal
(*M. stellatum*)

DESCRIPTION: Herbaceous perennials 1–4 ft tall, growing from thick, whitish, branching rhizomes, often found in dense clusters. Leaves alternate along the stems in 2 rows, 2–6 in long, broad, elliptic, smooth-edged, distinctly parallel-veined, often clasping. Flowers small, cream-colored, 6-parted, in dense, terminal clusters. Grows in rich woods, thickets and moist clearings throughout our area.

False Solomon's-seal (*M. racemosum*) grows in clumps to 4 ft tall from a fleshy, stout rootstock. Stems unbranching, arching. Flowers in clusters of 50–70. Berries at first green with copper spots, ripening to red, often with purple spots, in tight clusters. Inhabits moist forests and open woodlands from sea level to middle elevations throughout our area. Also called: feathery false lily-of-the-valley • *Smilacina racemosa.*

Star-flowered false Solomon's-seal (*M. stellatum*) grows to 20 in tall. Flowers in clusters of 5–6. Berries at first green with thin, blue-purple stripes that expand to cover the fruit when ripe. Smaller than false Solomon's-seal, with fewer flowers and leaves, and a lot fewer, larger berries (2–8). Found throughout Washington and Oregon. Also called: starry false lily-of-the-valley • *Smilacina stellata.*

183

Fairybells   *Prosartes* spp.

Rough-fruited fairybells (*P. trachycarpa*)

The berries of these species were not widely named or eaten by Native Americans, and reports vary greatly as to whether the fruit of fairybells is edible or not, so caution is advised. Vague ethnographic records for our area indicate that a few tribes in Washington considered fairybells poisonous, whereas others used them as a love medicine (such is life!). Not far away, the Thompson and Shuswap in British Columbia and the Blackfoot in Montana ate the berries raw. Rough-fruited fairybells were called "false raspberries" in the Shuswap language. Some reports describe the fruit of Hooker's fairybells as somewhat sweet-tasting and juicy, but growing so sparsely as not to warrant the effort to gather them. The berries of rough-fruited fairybells have been described as distinctly apricot flavored.

Fairybells were associated with ghosts or snakes by the Lummi and other Native Americans. Common indigenous names for these fruits include "snake berries" and "grizzly bear's favorite food," and rodents and grouse are known to feed on them. The leaves of fairybells are "drip tips," a form that ingeniously channels rainwater to the base of the plant.

EDIBILITY: edible with caution

Hooker's fairybells (*P. hookeri*)

FRUIT: Egg-shaped, orange or yellow to bright red berries.

SEASON: Flowers April to July. Fruit ripens July.

SPECIES DESCRIPTION: Perennial herbs 12–36 in tall, with few branches, from thick-spreading rhizomes. Leaves alternate, broadly oval, 1–4 in long, prominently parallel-veined, pointed at tip, rounded to heart-shaped base. Flowers creamy to greenish white, narrowly bell-shaped, ⅜–¾ in long, drooping, 1–3 at branch tips. Grows in moist woods, forests and thickets, as well as in subalpine meadows.

Hooker's fairybells (*P. hookeri*) has smooth, finely haired berries with 4–6 large seeds. Leaves sparsely hairy above and strongly hairy below. Found in all forested parts of our region. Also called: Oregon fairybells • *Disporum hookeri*.

Largeflower fairybells (*P. smithii*) is distinguished by its long, white petals that obscure the stamens. Stems up to 36 in tall, usually branched. Leaves, stems and fruit are smooth and lack hairs. Found in low-elevation, wet forests from the Olympic Peninsula south throughout western Oregon and

sporadically in Wallowa County. Also called: Smith's fairybells • *D. smithii*.

Rough-fruited fairybells (*P. trachycarpa*) has stems with few branches and grows to 24 in tall. Leaves sparsely hairy below and hairless above. Stamens hang well below the flower petals. Berries orange to red, conspicuously rough-skinned with velvety surface; seeds 6–12. Found in north-central and eastern Washington and eastern Oregon. Also called: *D. trachycarpum*.

Largeflower fairybells (*P. smithii*)

Rough-fruited fairybells (*P. trachycarpa*)

185

Strawberries _Fragaria_ spp.

Woodland strawberry (_F. vesca_)

These delicious little berries pack significantly more flavor than the typical large, domestic strawberries. Wild strawberries are small compared to modern cultivars and are probably best enjoyed as a nibble along the trail, but they can also be collected for use in desserts and beverages. A handful of bruised berries or leaves steeped in hot water makes a delicious tea and can be served either hot or cold.

Strawberries are popular among Native Americans, but their juiciness can make them difficult to dry and preserve. Today, strawberries are prepared by freezing, canning or making jam, but they were traditionally sun-dried. The berries were mashed and spread over grass or mats to dry in cakes, which were later eaten dry or rehydrated, either alone or mixed as a sweetener with other foods. Anyone who has had the extreme pleasure of savoring dried wild strawberries knows that this is a treat well worth the time to prepare! Strawberry flowers, leaves and stems were sometimes mixed with roots in cooking pits as a flavoring.

Strawberries contain many quickly assimilated minerals, including sodium, calcium, potassium, iron, sulfur and silicon, as well as citric and malic acids, and they were traditionally prescribed to enrich the blood. Strawberry-leaf tea, accompanied by fresh strawberries, was recommended as a remedy remedy for gout, rheumatism and inflamed mucous membranes, as well as for liver, kidney and gallbladder problems. Strawberries are a good source of ellagic acid, a chemical that is believed to prevent cancer. To remove tartar and whiten discolored teeth, strawberry juice can be held in the mouth for a few minutes, and then rinsed off the teeth with warm water. This treatment is reported to be most effective with a pinch of baking soda in the water. Large amounts of this fruit in the diet also appear to slow dental plaque

Virginia strawberry (*F. virginiana*)

Virginia strawberry (*F. virginiana*)

Woodland strawberry (*F. vesca*)

formation. Strawberry juice rubbed into the skin and later rinsed off with warm water has been used to soothe and heal sunburn.

Many people will be surprised to learn that the strawberry is technically *not* a fruit! What we think of as the "berry" is actually a swollen receptacle (the base of the flower, which you would normally expect to see inside a fruit). The true "fruits" are the tiny, dark seeds, called achenes, that you see either embedded in or perched on the soft flesh of the strawberry.

Virginia strawberry and beach strawberry are the original parents of 90 percent of our modern cultivated strawberry varieties.

EDIBILITY: highly edible

FRUIT: Berries are red when ripe, resembling miniature cultivated strawberries.

Season: Flowers May to August. Fruit ripens starting in June. Flowers continue to bloom throughout the season, so plants often have ripe fruit and flowers at the same time.

Description: Low, creeping perennials with long, slender runners (stolons). Leaves green, 2–4 in across, with 3 sharply toothed leaflets, often turning red in fall. Flowers white, 5-petaled, ½–1 in across, usually several per stem, forming small, loose clusters.

Beach strawberry (*F. chiloensis*) has green, thick, leathery leaflets, net-veined, wrinkled above and hairy

Virginia strawberry (*F. virginiana*)

Virginia strawberry (*F. virginiana*)

Beach strawberry (*F. chiloensis*)

below, with the end tooth shorter than adjacent teeth. Plants produce hairy runners. Found only along the coast on dunes, in rock crevices and on sea bluffs and beaches. Also called: coastal strawberry.

Virginia strawberry (*F. virginiana*) has bluish green leaflets, with the end tooth narrower and shorter than adjacent teeth. More common east of the Cascades in dry to moist, open woodlands and clearings, often in disturbed areas on well-drained sites

in prairie to subalpine zones, but occasionally found west of the Cascades. Also called: wild strawberry, common strawberry.

Woodland strawberry (*F. vesca*) has yellowish green leaflets, with the end tooth projecting beyond the adjacent teeth. Leaflets thick, hairy, strongly veined and scalloped. Common in dry to moist, open woods and meadows and on streambanks throughout our area.

Woodland strawberry (*F. vesca*)

Virginia strawberry (*F. virginiana*)

Wild Berry Muffins

Makes 12 muffins

This batter can also be baked in a loaf form.

5 Tbsp vegetable oil · 2 eggs, lightly beaten
1½ cups mixed wild berries (strawberries, thimbleberries, blueberries, huckleberries, etc.)
1 tsp salt · 1¾ cups whole wheat flour
¾ cup brown sugar · 2¼ tsp baking powder

Preheat oven to 400°F. Mix wet ingredients together in a bowl. Sift dry ingredients together in another bowl. Make a shallow well in the centre of the dry ingredients and slowly add the wet mixture. Mix well and pour into greased or lined muffin tins. Bake for 10 to 15 minutes, or until a knife inserted into a muffin comes out clean.

Brittle Prickly Pear *Opuntia fragilis*

Brittle prickly pear (*O. fragilis*)

The fruit and flesh of many prickly pear species are eaten throughout the world. The Colville traditionally roasted the newly formed stems of brittle prickly pear to remove the sharp spines so that the flesh could be safely eaten. Columbia prickly pear can be prepared in the same way, and eastern prickly pear, which is native to eastern North America and also found in the Willamette Valley, has edible pads as well as juicy fruit that can be eaten fresh or made into jelly. The flower petals of all prickly pears are edible and are said to have a sweet taste. Reportedly, prickly pear was a food valued by older men because it helped them urinate more easily. Although the spines are often cursed by hasty harvesters, they were traditionally used to pierce ears, make fish hooks and armor poles supporting food caches.

EDIBILITY: stem flesh and flower petals edible; fruit of our 2 common species too dry to be eaten

FRUIT: Green, pear-shaped fruits (tunas) with a few spines or bristles, to 1 in long, dry with a few large seeds, often sterile.

SEASON: Flowers in late spring. Fruit ripens through late summer and fall.

DESCRIPTION: Mat-forming cactus with well-armored, green stems sectioned into pear-shaped segments 1–2 in long and nearly as wide that easily detach (as the name *fragilis* suggests). Leaves scale-like, falling off early in the season. Spines brownish, about 1 in long, in clusters of 2–7. Flowers 1–2 in across, numerous yellow petals, solitary, arising from a bristly, white-haired cushion. Found in dry, open areas, usually in sandy soil, in northern and central Washington and eastern Oregon.

Columbia prickly pear (*O. × columbiana*) is a hybrid (*O. fragilis × polyacantha*) and has many of the same features as brittle prickly pear but with slightly flattened stem segments and larger flowers (2–3 in wide) that are sometimes red or red-tinged. Fruit greenish, dry and pear-shaped. Found on the plains throughout the Columbia Plateau. Also called: *O. polyacantha.*

Eastern prickly pear (*O. humifusa*) is native to eastern North America but has been reported in the Willamette Valley. It is larger than brittle prickly pear, with strongly flattened stems covered with barbed bristles but lacking stiff spines. Fruit red, 1–2 in long, juicy, edible.

Brittle prickly pear (*O. fragilis*)

Brittle prickly pear (*O. fragilis*)

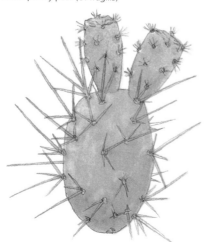

Eastern prickly pear (*O. humifusa*)

Groundcherries & Wild Tomatoes *Physalis* spp.

Longleaf groundcherry (*P. longifolia*)

Groundcherries and wild tomatoes are a poorly known group of herbaceous perennials and annuals in the same family as tomatoes and nightshades. Most species produce edible fruit, and preliminary (preclinical) research has shown that the fruit of longleaf groundcherry contains over a dozen compounds that show potent anti-cancer activity in melanomas, brain tumors and thyroid and breast cancers, as well as head and neck squamous cell cancers, without any side effects.

Native Americans east of our region traditionally ate the fruit of longleaf groundcherry and clammy groundcherry, as well as husk tomato.

These fruits were enjoyed fresh, cooked into sauces or dried for use during the winter. All of the groundcherries and wild tomatoes in our area have been introduced and grow as weeds. The leaves of all species are toxic and should not be eaten.

Physalis is Greek for "bladder" and refers to the sack-like husk.

EDIBILITY: ripe fruit edible with flavors described as similar to tomatoes or strawberries, sour to slightly bitter in some species

FRUIT: Tomato-like, green to orange or red berries ⅜–½ in wide, each enclosed in a papery, lantern-like husk.

SEASON: Flowers June to September. Fruit ripens July to October.

DESCRIPTION: Upright perennials and annuals 1–10 ft tall, similar in appearance to a garden tomato. Flowers bell-shaped with 5 fused petals and often dark spots on the inside.

WARNING: *Unripe berries, leaves and roots of these species may be toxic and should not be eaten.*

Clammy groundcherry (*P. heterophylla*) is a perennial herb growing from a thick rhizome. Stems up to 20 in tall and covered with gland-tipped hairs. Leaves alternate, oval, 2–5 in long, heart-shaped at the base, covered with gland-tipped hairs, with petioles 1/2 in long. Flowers yellow with purple center, 1 in wide, drooping. Fruit orange, 1 in wide, inside a green to brown husk. Fruit slightly bitter-tasting but edible; all other parts of the plant are poisonous. Grows as a weed in eastern Washington.

Clammy groundcherry (*P. heterophylla*)

Clammy groundcherry (*P. heterophylla*)

Longleaf groundcherry (*P. longifolia*)

Husk tomato (*P. pubescens*) is an annual herb with a densely gland-tipped, hairy stem reaching 2 ft tall. Leaves oval to heart-shaped, 1–4 in long, with either smooth or toothed margins. Flowers yellow with 5 dark spots on the inside, axillary, bell-shaped, ³/₈ in long. Husk ⁵/₈–1¹/₂ in long, green maturing to tan. Fruit ¹/₂ in wide, greenish orange when ripe. Found in disturbed areas in western Oregon, growing as an introduced weed. Also called: hairy groundcherry.

Longleaf groundcherry (*P. longifolia*) is a perennial from a rhizome. Stems 8–24 in long, hairless or with straight, stiff, inconspicuous hairs. Leaves 2–3 in long, oval to lance-shaped, smooth or wavy margins, mostly hairless, long-stalked. Flowers ¹/₂–³/₄ in wide, yellow with purple spots or veins in the center. Husk spade-shaped, green maturing to greenish tan. Fruit ³/₈ in wide, green when ripe. Grows on dry, rocky roadsides along the Snake River in northeastern Oregon and southeastern Washington.

Mexican groundcherry (*P. philadelphica*) is a hairless or sparsely glandular-haired annual growing to 3 ft tall. Leaves 2–3 inches long, oval, with margins either smooth or toothed. Flowers green with purple veins and 5 dark purple spots on the inside. Fruit green, ³/₈–2 in wide, completely filling or splitting the husk at maturity. The fruit is widely grown as a food crop, and plants occasionally escape cultivation. Also called: tomatillo.

Husk tomato (*P. pubescens*)

Longleaf groundcherry (*P. longifolia*)

Prairie groundcherry (*P. hispida*) is a perennial growing to 16 in tall. Both bud clusters and ripe fruit are reported to be edible. Very little has been published about this species. Also called: *P. lanceolata*.

Strawberry-tomato (*P. grisea*) is an introduced species sometimes considered a variety of husk tomato by taxonomists. Leaves 2–4 inches long. Flowers smaller and petals shorter than those of husk tomato.

Mexican groundcherry (*P. philadelphica*)

195

Nightshades · *Solanum* spp.

American black nightshade (*S. americanum*)

American black nightshade and European black nightshade were formerly lumped together under the scientific name *Solanum nigrum*, making it impossible to attribute ethnobotanical accounts to one species or the other. The fully ripe berries of one or perhaps both species were eaten by the Tübatulabal and other Native Americans in northern California, but some groups in Mendocino County considered unripe berries to be poisonous. Farther north in the Klamath area, the Karuk also regarded unripe berries as toxic. The Cherokee relished the young leaves (before flowering) as a potherb. Both the cooked greens and ripe fruit are widely eaten as a traditional food throughout the world. Perhaps because of the English common name "deadly nightshade," which is an alternate name for the undisputedly poisonous

Silverleaf nightshade (*S. elaeagnifolium*)

belladonna *(Atropa bella-donna)*, pp. 230–31, there are conflicting accounts of the edibility of black nightshades among non-native North Americans as well. Foraging expert Sam Thayer devotes considerable attention to debunking the myth that European and American black nightshade are poisonous in his book *Nature's Garden*.

The ripe berries of cutleaf nightshade were eaten by the Acoma and Laguna in times of food shortages. The Zuni mixed the boiled fruit with ground chili and salt as a condiment.

Seven species are described below and an additional species, climbing nightshade (*S. dulcamara*), is covered on pp. 228–29 in the Poisonous Berries section. A few more weedy species are found rarely in Oregon and are not included.

Solanum means "quieting" in Latin, a reference to the narcotic properties of some species.

EDIBILITY: 2 species with edible ripe fruit, 4 not recommended, 1 poisonous species (climbing nightshade, *S. dulcamara*); all should be regarded with caution unless harvesters are confident in their ability to differentiate nightshade species and identify toxic belladonna (*Atropa bella-donna*)

FRUIT: Round, green to black berries ⅓–½ in wide, in clumps of 2–7 or more.

SEASON: Flowers as early as May but most species flower July to October. Fruit ripens throughout late summer and fall.

DESCRIPTION: Herbaceous annuals and perennials with reclining or ascending stalks to 3 ft tall. Leaves stalked (petiolate), alternate to nearly opposite, with smooth to deeply lobed margins. Flowers white or yellow, often dark-tinged toward the center, with yellow stamens; borne in umbel-like clusters in many of our species.

American black nightshade (*S. americanum*) is part of the *S. nigrum* complex and is only slightly different than European black nightshade. Flowers July to August and produces fruit a few weeks later. Ripe fruit edible. Introduced from more southern parts of the Americas. Found in disturbed areas, roadsides and open areas on both sides of the Cascades in Washington and Oregon.

Carolina nightshade (*S. carolinense*) is a few-branched, perennial herb 1–3 ft tall, with a spiny stem. Leaves

American black nightshade (*S. americanum*)

2–6 in long, with wavy to lobed margins that resemble black nightshade, but are wider and lobed. Flowers light purple or white. Fruits ⅜–1 in wide, yellow, resembling tomatoes. Toxic alkaloids are concentrated in the leaves and roots, but less so in the fruit, which is not always considered poisonous in the literature; not recommended for consumption. Introduced from the southeastern U.S. and weedy in southeastern Washington and eastern Oregon. Also called: Carolina horsenettle.

Cutleaf nightshade (*S. triflorum*) is a slightly hairy, herbaceous annual, with stems 4–24 in long, sprawling along the ground. Leaves 1–2 in long with deep, oak leaf–like lobes. Flowers white with yellow anthers, in few-flowered clusters. Berries greenish,

about ½ in wide. Little is known about the edibility of the fruit; not recommended for consumption. Introduced in eastern Washington and Oregon.

European black nightshade (*S. nigrum*) is a smooth-stemmed annual with a branched stem reaching 2 ft tall. Leaves 1–3 in long, ovate to triangular-tipped, upper and lower surfaces either hairy or hairless, and margins either smooth, wavy or with a few blunt teeth. Flowers white to faintly bluish, with 5 unequal lobes, 5 yellow stamens, in small, drooping clusters. Blooms July to October. Berries ⅜ in wide, green maturing to black, in clusters of few to several. Ripe fruit edible. Introduced from Europe. Found on roadsides and in disturbed areas on both sides of the Cascades.

Hoe nightshade (*S. physalifolium*) is an herbaceous, taprooted annual with a branching stem reaching 2 ft tall and

Carolina nightshade (*S. carolinese*)

Cutleaf nightshade (*S. triflorum*)

covered with soft, sticky hairs. Leaves 1–3 in long, ovate to deltoid, with smooth margins or a few blunt teeth. Flowers white with yellow anthers, in few-flowered clusters on ascending stalks. Berries yellowish or greenish, about ⅜ in wide, eaten by the Piute as a treatment for diarrhea. Little is known about the edibility of the fruit; not recommended for consumption. Introduced from South America to disturbed and open areas throughout our region.

Parish's nightshade (*S. parishii*) is a perennial herb with a ribbed stem ascending to 3 ft tall. Leaves oval to lance-shaped, up to 3 inches long,

Parish's nightshade (*S. parishii*)

Hoe nightshade (*S. physalifolium*)

Parish's nightshade (*S. parishii*)

with smooth or wavy margins. Flowers purple with yellow anthers, about 1 in wide. Blooms May and June. Berries green, $\frac{1}{4}$–$\frac{3}{8}$ in wide. Edibility unknown; not recommended for consumption. Native to our area and found in southwestern Oregon in oak and pine forests, as well as chaparral.

Silverleaf nightshade (*S. elaeagnifolium*) is a prickly stemmed herbaceous perennial that reaches 3 ft tall. Both leaves and stems are densely covered with fine, soft hairs, giving the plant a silvery appearance. Leaves 2–6 in long, $\frac{1}{4}$–1 inch in wide, margins smooth, wavy. Flowers star-shaped, blue to light purple with yellow stamens. Berries yellow-red, persisting on the plant through winter. This species is poisonous. It contains the solanine, which causes stomach, heart and neurological problems, as well as solanidine, a steroidal alkaloid useful for modern hormone synthesis. Several Native American groups in the desert Southwest traditionally use the berries and roots medicinally and the powdered berries in cheese making. Likely introduced from the desert Southwest as it is only recorded in our area in northeastern Oregon.

> **WARNING:** *Many* Solanum *species have toxic vegetation and berries. Be sure of your identification! Those species with edible berries may be toxic if the berries are not fully ripe.*

Silverleaf nightshade (*S. elaeagnifolium*)

American black nightshade (*S. americanum*)

Wolfberry *Lycium barbarum*

Also called: goji berry, matrimony vine

Wolfberry (*L. barbarum*)

Another member of the nightshade family, wolfberry is highly sought after by health-conscious people as a "superfood" because of the fruit's high levels of nutrients and beneficial phytochemicals, many acting as antioxidants. One hundred grams (about 3½ oz) of dried wolfberries contain 9 mg of iron, 50 mcg of selenium, 1.3 mg of vitamin B2, 29–148 mg of vitamin C, 7 mg of betacarotene and 2.4–200 mg of zeaxanthin, a compound thought to help prevent eye disorders.

Wolfberries are most commonly imported to the United States as a dried fruit and sold under the name "goji berry" or "Tibetan goji berry." Companies promoting wolfberries have claimed that a Chinese man named Li Qing Yuen ate the berries daily and lived to the age of 252! Maybe that is why they are so expensive. No matter—these plants are escaping cultivation and growing like weeds the drier parts of our region.

EDIBILITY: highly edible; cultivated in China and the United Kingdom

FRUIT: Bright orange berries, ⅜–¾ in long and half as wide, with smooth, shiny skin and numerous yellow seeds.

SEASON: Flowers June to September. Fruit ripens August to November.

DESCRIPTION: Sparsely thorny, deciduous, woody shrub or vine that grows to 15 ft tall. Leaves alternate along the stalk, lanceolate to ovate, up to 3 in long and half as wide, occasionally in clumps of 2–3, on short petioles. Flowers pink to purple, with 5–6 petals, hanging in clusters of 1–3 from leaf axils. Introduced from Asia to our area, where it is mostly found east of the Cascades in disturbed sites.

203

California Greenbrier *Smilax californica*

California greenbrier (*S. californica*)

Native Americans valued California greenbrier mainly as a basketry material on account of its long, flexible vines, which become woody with age. The tender young shoots and tendrils of some *Smilax* species in eastern North America are edible, but little is known about the edibility of California greenbrier.

A few Chinese species even have edible fruits and tuberous roots. An extract from a Jamaican species (as well as a few others) is used to make a type of sarsaparilla root beer. One source claims that the roots of our species can be used to make a gelatinous flour.

The name *Smilax* comes to us from the Greek myth of Krokus, a tragedy about a mortal man who falls in love with a wood nymph named Smilax. In the myth, the gods transformed Krokus into a flower, the crocus, and Smilax into a brier because the two lovers were unhappy.

EDIBILITY: berries not recommended; other plant parts unknown; tubers and young shoots may be edible

FRUIT: Black berries ¼ in wide.

SEASON: Flowers May to June. Fruit ripens mid- to late summer.

DESCRIPTION: Perennial, climbing or trailing, prickly vine. Leaves alternate, 2–4 in long, smooth to wavy-margined, heart-shaped base, pointed to hooked tip; 2 unbranched tendrils grow from each leaf stalk. Flowers light green, in compact clusters of 12–24, hanging on long stalks from leaf axils. Grows along streamsides in coniferous forests from low to middle elevations in southwestern Oregon.

Spikenards *Aralia* spp.

California spikenard (*A. californicus*)

Spikenards have a variety of medicinal uses. Native Americans in northern California used the roots of California spikenard to reduce fever, treat lung problems, cure gastric issues and decrease swelling. A root concoction of small spikenard was similarly used by the Bella Bella to treat stomach complaints, and it was taken by many Native Americans across the continent to strengthen the blood. Although the fruit is eaten by birds and bears, the foliage browsed by deer and caribou, and the roots eaten by rabbits, there is little ethnographic evidence in our area that spikenards were eaten by humans. However, on the central coast of British Columbia the Kwakwaka'wakw roasted and ate the roots of small spikenard with fish oil, and farther north, the Nuxalk boiled the roots to make a beverage. Elsewhere throughout North America,

Small spikenard (*A. nudicaulis*)

small spikenard roots and berries were used by Native Americans and settlers to make wine and flavor root beer.

EDIBILITY: not recommended as food but an important medicinal

FRUIT: Dark purple to black, round berries, ¼ in wide, in tightly packed, spherical clusters, often 2 or more clusters per branching stalk.

SEASON: Flowers June and July. Fruit ripens August and September.

DESCRIPTION: Upright perennial herbs 1–9 ft tall with compound leaves. Leaflets egg- to lance-shaped with acuminate tips and serrated margins. Flowers small, in 3 to many tight umbels arranged along a branched flowering stalk. Usually found in damp, rich soils in shaded forests.

California spikenard (*A. californica*) is a large perennial herb that grows 6–9 ft tall. Leaves compound, pinnately divided 1–3 times into leaflets 6–12 in long with serrated margins and heart-shaped bases. Flowers white, in tight umbels on an upright, many-branched stalk 12–18 in long. Berries black, round, up to ¼ in wide. Found along streambanks in moist, shaded forests at low to middle elevations in the Klamath Mountains and south-western Oregon. Also called: California aralia, elk clover.

Small spikenard (*A. nudicaulis*) is a perennial herb that grows from a spreading rhizome. Stems grow straight out of the ground and divide into 3 branches, each with 3–7 compound, pinnately divided leaves 12–30 in long. Leaflets 2–5 in long, oval, with long tips and serrated margins. Flowers numerous, small, greenish white, in usually 3–7 umbels (spherical clusters), the flower stalks sometimes hidden by the leaves. Berries dark purple, ¼ in wide or slightly larger. Grows in damp, shaded areas in northeastern Washington. Also called: wild sarsaparilla.

Small spikenard (*A. nudicaulis*)

Bastard Toadflax *Comandra umbellata*

Bastard toadflax (*C. umbellata*)

Bastard toadflax is a small plant that is easy to overlook. Foresters vilify this plant because it frequently parasitizes the roots of species in the aster and rose families, as well as a few trees. It is also the alternate host for comandra blister rust, which kills the tops of pine trees in North America. However, the seeds were eaten by the Okanagon and Paiute, and children also enjoyed sipping the sweet nectar of the flowers. Bastard toadflax can efficiently assimilate selenium from the soil. Selenium is an important antioxidant but can also be toxic in large doses. However, soil selenium levels are generally deficient in Washington and Oregon, causing major losses to livestock owners in our area. Nevertheless, prolonged consumption of large quantities of bastard toadflax fruit is not recommended.

EDIBILITY: edible with caution

FRUIT: Round, purple to brown berries with dry to juicy flesh.

SEASON: Flowers April to August. Fruit ripens late July to September.

DESCRIPTION: Smooth-stemmed, hairless perennial herb that often parasitizes the roots of other plants but is still capable of photosynthesis. Stems upright, clustered, 2–12 in tall. Leaves alternate along the stalk, lance-shaped, less than 2 in long, green to whitish green. Flowers white, 5-petaled, in terminal clusters. Hosts include herbs such as asters, shrubs such as roses and huckleberries, and trees such as maples and birches. Found on well-drained, moist soils mostly east of the Cascades in Washington and throughout non-coastal Oregon.

False toadflax (*Geocaulon lividum*) is another herbaceous perennial that parasitizes roots. Stems to 12 in tall. Leaves alternate, oval to oblong, thin. Flowers greenish or purple, in cluster of 1–4 in leaf axils. Berries fleshy, orange, with 1 seed. Found only in northeastern Washington in our area. Although the berries are edible and eaten by Native Americans in Alaska, they are best left alone in our region because false toadflax is on the Washington State Conservation watch-list. Also called: *Comandra livida*.

False toadflax (*Geocaulon lividum*)

False toadflax (*Geocaulon lividum*)

Bastard toadflax (*C. umbellata*)

False toadflax (*Geocaulon lividum*)

Cascara, Buckthorn, Redberry & Coffeeberry   *Rhamnus* spp. and *Frangula* spp.

Holly-leaved redberry (*R. ilicifolia*)

Some sources report that native peoples ate the red or purple berries of these small trees or shrubs, but it was most likely in modest amounts given their strong purgative action. Other sources consider the fruits of these species poisonous. The berries have been described as bland to bitter in taste and should not generally be considered edible.

These species have been used as laxatives for at least hundreds of years (and probably longer given Native American historic use), and they are highly regarded because their action is

Cascara (*R. purshiana*)

fairly gentle and not habit-forming. Indigenous peoples collected the bark in spring and summer, then dried and stored it for later use. The dried bark was traditionally used to make medicinal teas, but today, it is usually administered as a liquid extract or elixir, or in tablet form. Each year, 500–4000 tons of cascara bark are collected commercially, mainly from wild trees in British Columbia, Washington, Oregon and California.

EDIBILITY: edible with caution, considered toxic

FRUIT: Berry-like drupes, red, purple or black, $^{3}/_{16}$–$^{9}/_{16}$ in wide, often ripening unevenly in bunches.

SEASON: Flowers June to July. Fruit ripens August to September.

DESCRIPTION: Erect or spreading, deciduous shrubs or small trees 1–35 ft tall. Leaves alternate, $^{1}/_{2}$–6 in long, glossy, oval to elliptic, usually prominently veined, margins smooth to spiny-toothed. Flowers inconspicuous, greenish yellow, 5-petaled, all male, all female or mixed in flat-topped clusters of up to 25 flowers, in leaf axils. Grows along streamsides and in open- to closed-canopy forests at low to montane elevations on both sides of the Cascades in Washington and in western, northeastern and south-central Oregon.

Alderleaf buckthorn (*R. alnifolia*) is a shrub less than 6 ft tall with gray bark and brown twigs. Leaves alternate, 2–5 inches long, thin, with narrow tips, irregularly toothed margins and prominent, curved veins. Flowers 5-petaled, in clusters of 1–3 on short stalks. Fruit $^{5}/_{16}$ in wide, black

Alderleaf buckthorn (*R. alnifolia*)

when ripe. Grows in wet, open forests, wet meadows and on streamsides. Uncommon at high elevations in northeastern Washington and northeastern and south-central Oregon. Also called: alderleaf coffeeberry.

Cascara (*R. purshiana*) Erect or spreading, deciduous shrub or small tree to 35 ft tall. Bark smooth, gray, bitter-tasting. Leaves alternate, 2–6 in long, glossy, oval to elliptic, prominently veined, margins smooth or

> **WARNING:** *Some sources consider the fruits of these species poisonous. These genera contain large amounts of anthraquinones, which are responsible for their emetic properties. Ingesting fresh bark and berries can have severe effects, but curing the bark for at least one year or using a heat treatment reduces the harshness.*

finely toothed, turning a pretty yellow color in fall. Flowers inconspicuous, greenish yellow, 5-petaled, all male or all female in a single stalked cluster, forming flat-topped clusters of up to 25 flowers in leaf axils, blooming April to June. Fruit 1/4–3/8 in wide, ripening from greenish red to purplish black from mid-July to September. Grows on streamsides and in open- to closed-canopy forests at low to montane elevations on both sides of the Cascades in Washington and in western, northeastern and south-central Oregon.

Holly-leaved redberry (*R. ilicifolia*) is similar to California buckthorn but is a sprawling shrub less than 12 ft tall. Leaves evergreen, holly-like, 1–2 in long. Fruits red, 3/16–3/8 in wide. A sensitive species limited in our area to Jackson County, Oregon.

California buckthorn (*F. californica* ssp. *occidentalis*) is a larger shrub, growing to 15 ft tall, with gray to light brown bark and finely haired twigs. Leaves evergreen, thick, 1–3 in long. Flowers cream-colored, in tight umbels, blooming in June. Fruit 3/8–9/16 in wide, purple, ripening in July and August. Range limited to moderate elevations in chaparral and woodlands in southwestern Oregon. Also called: western California coffeeberry • *R. californica*.

Sierra coffeeberry (*F. rubra*) is a small shrub less than 6 ft tall. Leaves deciduous, 1/2–3 in long, lacking prominent veins. Fruit 1/2 in wide, greenish yellow ripening to dark purple. Found in southwestern Oregon.

California buckthorn (*R. californica* ssp. *occidentalis*)

Sierra coffeeberry (*R. rubra*)

Cascara (*R. purshiana*)

213

English Holly *Ilex aquifolium*

English holly (*I. aquifolium*)

Introduced from Eurasia, this species is a common garden and municipal ornamental throughout the Pacific Northwest. Its bright red berries are a traditional symbol of the Christmas holidays; indeed, British Columbia has a thriving holly export industry that sends sprigs of leaves and berries to the rest of Canada and parts of the U.S., and there is potential for harvesting and selling the holly greenery from our region as well. Considered a threat to Garry oak and Douglas-fir ecosystems, there is little to check the spread of English holly into natural areas because its spiky leaves are well-protected from browsing, and the seeds are spread far and wide by the birds such as robins, which love eating the berries.

EDIBILITY: poisonous

FRUIT: Round, berry-like drupes, to ³/₈ in across, shiny red (sometimes orange or yellow), containing 4 pits, in clusters that remain on the tree throughout winter and often well into spring.

SEASON: Flowers May. Fruit ripens September.

DESCRIPTION: Evergreen tree to 50 ft tall. Bark smooth, gray. Leaves alternate, to 5 in long, 1–3 in wide, glossy, leathery, variable in shape, often but not always with large, spiny teeth pointing alternately upward and downward. Flowers fragrant, bell-shaped, white or pale green, 4-petaled, to ¼ in long, in clusters. Male and female trees separate, with only females bearing fruit. Widespread throughout western Washington, the Willamette Valley and coastal Oregon, preferring moist forests, clearings and edges, but also inhabiting more marginal habitats such as dry forests.

WARNING: *Holly berries contain ilicin, a compound irritating to the intestines and the stomach, as well as harmful to the heart and nervous system. All holly berries are poisonous, and ingesting them can cause nausea, diarrhea and, in quantity (more than 20), can trigger violent vomiting or even death.*

Pacific Yew *Taxus brevifolia*

Also called: western yew, mountain mahogany

Pacific yew (*T. brevifolia*)

The bark of Pacific yew is the original source of the important anti-cancer drug Taxol. After a long period of development by the National Cancer Institute and pharmaceutical partners, this drug was approved for use in treating a variety of cancers and is particularly successful in treating breast and ovarian cancers that historically had extremely low survival rates.

The slow-growing Pacific yew, however, became quickly depleted in the wild by unregulated overharvesting. There are ongoing concerns regarding its natural regeneration because for many years, it was considered a "weedy" species in second-growth timber stands and was removed. It also requires both a male and a female tree growing in relatively close proximity to reproduce.

Taxane derivatives are now in great part obtained from managed harvest of the more common Canada yew (*T. canadensis*) in eastern Canada, from which the drug is prepared by extraction and semi-synthesis. Some native peoples used yew bark for treating illness; indeed, this is how modern researchers first knew to investigate this plant.

EDIBILITY: edible with extreme caution, poisonous

FRUIT: Berry-like arils, ⅛–³/₁₆ in across, with a cup of orange to red, fleshy tissue around a single, bony seed. The showy, berry-like fruit of this species, with its sweet taste but slimy texture, has historically been considered edible. However, the hard seeds found within the fleshy cup are extremely poisonous, so this fruit is not recommended for consumption (see Warning).

SEASON: Flowers June. Fruit ripens August to October.

DESCRIPTION: Small, generally scraggly looking evergreen shrub or tree with a straight trunk, growing to 50 ft tall (rarely to 75 ft). Branches drooping. Bark reddish brown, scaly, flaking. Needles soft, flattened, 1½ in long, arranged alternately in 2 rows, sharp-tipped, glossy green above, paler green beneath with 2 whitish bands of stomata. Trees are male or female and often grow together in small thickets. Male pollen-bearing cones inconspicuous; tiny, green flowers of female trees eventually produce scarlet red arils. Unusually, this conifer has no pitch. Grows in moist, shady sites such as along streambanks and in mature coniferous forests, at low to montane elevations.

WARNING: *The needles, bark and seeds contain extremely poisonous, heart-depressing alkaloids called taxanes. Drinking yew tea or eating as few as 50 leaves can cause death. Many birds eat the berries, which take 2 years to mature. The branches are said to be a preferred winter browse for moose, but many horses, cattle, sheep, goats, pigs and deer have been poisoned from eating yew shrubs, especially when the branches were previously cut.*

217

Black Twinberry

Lonicera involucrata

Also called: twinflower honeysuckle

Black twinberry (*L. involucrata*)

Black twinberry's shiny, black berries were not eaten by Native Americans and were considered poisonous by many. On the Pacific coast, where the berries acquired names such as "raven's food" and "monster food," there were some taboos against eating them. However, wildlife such as ravens, bears and crows eat them regularly, and a few reports claim that the berries are not harmful in small quantities. They taste very bitter, though, so are not very palatable.

This plant was mainly used medicinally. Twinberry bark was taken for coughs, and the leaves were chewed and applied externally to itchy skin, burns, inflammation, boils and gonorrheal sores. Berry tea was used as a cathartic and emetic as a means to purify the body and cleanse the stomach and chest. The small berries were also crushed and rubbed in the hair to cure dandruff.

Native Americans used the stems as building materials and to make fibers for mats, baskets, bags, blankets and toys. Children used the hollow stems as toys. A black dye was obtained from the crushed berries and used for basketry materials.

Black twinberry is resistant to air pollution and is sometimes planted as an ornamental.

EDIBILITY: edible with caution, considered toxic

FRUIT: Shiny, black berries to ½ in across.

SEASON: Flowers May to July. Fruit ripens June to September.

DESCRIPTION: Deciduous, erect shrub to 15 ft tall. Twigs 4-angled, greenish when young, grayish with shredding bark when older. Leaves oval, to 6 in long and 3 in wide, sharp-pointed at tip. Flowers bell-shaped, yellow, ½–1 in long, in pairs surrounded by fused bracts (an "involucre," hence the scientific name *involucrata*). Grows in moist or wet

soil in forests, clearings, riverbanks, swamps and open woods. Found at low to middle elevations throughout the forested parts of Washington and Oregon.

Poison-ivy & Poison-oak *Toxicodendron* spp.

Pacific poison-oak (*T. diversilobum*)

Poison-ivy and poison-oak plants contain an oily resin called urushiol that causes a nasty skin reaction in most people, especially on sensitive skin and mucous membranes. Because the skin reaction appears with some delay after exposure, many people do not realize that they have come into contact with these plants until it is too late. Sensitization can also lead to a more severe reaction after repeated exposure.

Urushiol is not volatile and is therefore not transmitted through the air, but it can be carried to unsuspecting victims on pets, clothing and tools, and even on smoke particles from burning poison-ivy or poison-oak plants.

The resin can persist on pets and clothing for months and is also ejected in fine droplets into the air when the plants are pulled from the soil.

Washing with a strong soap can prevent a reaction if it is done shortly after contact because this process can remove the urushiol resin. Washing also prevents transfer of the resin to other parts of the body or to other people. Be sure to use cold water because warm water can help the resin penetrate your skin, where it is extremely difficult to remove. The liquid that oozes from poison-ivy or poison-oak blisters on affected skin does not contain the allergen. Ointments and even household ammonia

Western poison-ivy (*T. rydbergii*)

Western poison-ivy (*T. rydbergii*)

Pacific poison-oak (*T. diversilobum*)

can be used to relieve the itching in mild cases, but people with severe reactions might need to consult a doctor.

EDIBILITY: poisonous

FRUIT: Whitish to brown, berry-like drupes less than 1/4 in wide.

SEASON: Flowers May to June. Fruit ripens July to August.

DESCRIPTION: Trailing to erect, deciduous shrubs, forming colonies. Leaves bright green, glossy, resinous, compound, divided into 3 oval leaflets, turning scarlet in autumn. Flowers cream-colored, 5-petaled, 1/8 in across, in clusters. Plants either male or female.

Pacific poison-oak (*T. diversilobum*) grows to 6 ft tall. Leaflets round-tipped, usually lobed (hence the reference to "oak") and shorter than those of poison-ivy (to 3 in long vs. to 6 in or more in poison-ivy). Fruits whitish drupes. Grows on drier, rocky slopes at low elevations mostly west of the Cascades.

Western poison-ivy (*T. rydbergii*) grows to 6 ft tall and spreads mainly by stolons, forming distinct patches. Leaflets entire (neither toothed nor lobed), with pointed tip. A species of drier, rocky slopes, most commonly found east of the Cascades.

221

Devil's Club   *Oplopanax horridus*

Also called: *Echinopanax horridum*

Devil's club (*O. horridus*)

Throughout its range, devil's club, which is botanically a member of the ginseng family, is considered to be one of the most powerful and important of all medicinal plants. Native Americans in Washington and Oregon considered the berries of this plant to be inedible, perhaps partly because they are held aloft above a remarkable fortress of irritating, spiny leaves and stems and because even the berries have spikes! Although devil's club tea is recommended today for binge-eaters who are trying to lose weight, some tribes used it to improve appetite and to help people gain weight. In fact, it was said that a patient could gain too much weight if the plant was used for too long. Some tribes used a strong decoction of the plant to induce vomiting in purifying rituals preceding an important event such as a hunt or war expedition. This decoction was also applied to wounds to combat *Staphylococcus* infections, and ashes from burned stems were sometimes mixed with grease to make salves to heal swellings and weeping sores.

Like many members of the ginseng family, devil's club contains glycosides that are said to reduce metabolic stress and thus improve one's sense of well-being. The roots and bark contain the most active compounds and have traditionally been used to treat arthritis, diabetes, rheumatism, digestive troubles, gonorrhea and ulcers. The root tea reportedly stimulates the respiratory tract and helps bring up phlegm when treating colds, bronchitis and pneumonia. The tea has also been used to treat diabetes because it helps regulate blood sugar levels and reduce the craving for sugar. Indeed, devil's club extracts have successfully lowered blood sugar levels in laboratory animals.

Possibly because of its diabolical spines, devil's club was considered a highly powerful plant that could protect one from evil influences of many kinds. Devil's club sticks were used as protective charms, and charcoal from the burned plant was used to make protective face paint for dancers and others who were ritually vulnerable to evil influences. The Haida rubbed the bright red berries into their hair to combat dandruff and lice and to add shine. The Cowlitz pulverized the dried bark and used it as perfume and baby powder.

EDIBILITY: poisonous

FRUIT: Bright red, berry-like drupes, slightly flattened, sometimes spiny, ¼–⅓ in long, in showy, pyramidal, terminal clusters.

SEASON: Flowers May to July. Fruit ripens July to September.

DESCRIPTION: Strong-smelling deciduous shrub, 3–10 ft tall, with spiny, erect or sprawling stems. Leaves broadly maple-like, 4–16 in wide, with prickly ribs and long, bristly stalks. Spines on leaves and stems grow up to ⅜ in long. Flowers greenish white, ¼ in long, 5-petaled, in pyramidal clusters 4–10 in long. Grows in moist, shady foothill and montane sites. Easy to find when you lose your footing on a coastal trail as it is invariably the plant that you grab onto to stop your fall.

WARNING: *Devil's club spines are brittle and break off easily, embedding in the skin and causing infection. Some people have an allergic reaction to scratches from this plant. Wilted leaves can be toxic, so only fresh or completely dried leaves should be used to make medicinal tea, but even then, the tea should be taken under the guidance of a registered herbalist and in moderation because extended use can irritate the stomach and bowels.*

Snowberries *Symphoricarpos* spp.

Common snowberry (*S. albus*)

Although some sources report that common snowberries are edible, though not very good, they are somewhat toxic and can be mildly poisonous in large quantities. Most Native American groups considered snowberries poisonous and did not eat them but instead used them medicinally, though the Sqauxin reportedly consumed them. Some tribes believed that snowberries were the ghosts of serviceberries (*Amelanchier* spp.) and, because they were part of the spirit world, were not to be eaten by the living.

These spongy, white berries are fun to squish and pop—rather like bubble wrap! The unusual white berries persist on the plant through winter, providing a decorative display that in mild winters can last well into spring. The berries make a wonderful addition to winter holiday wreaths, garlands and other festive decorations. These are very drought-tolerant and decorative species that will thrive on steep slopes and in other areas that may otherwise be difficult to landscape. The leaves and flowers, albeit small, are pretty, and the white berries provide winter forage for birds and small mammals while giving a showy winter display.

Common snowberry is considered a management concern in Garry oak habitat because it quickly forms dense thickets that smother other plant species. Removing snowberry is difficult and labor intensive, and pulling out the dense root masses causes a great deal of soil disturbance and damage to surrounding plants. Because of its drought tolerance, tenacious roots and thick growth habit, however, it is ideal for stabilizing slopes and providing vegetation in difficult-to-plant areas.

Common snowberry (S. *albus*)

Common snowberry (S. *albus*)

EDIBILITY: edible with caution, poisonous in large quantities

FRUIT: White, waxy, spongy, berry-like drupes, ¼–⅝ in long, singly or in clusters at stem tips.

SEASON: Flowers May to August. Berries ripen and whiten August and September.

DESCRIPTION: Mostly erect shrubs (one trailing species) with opposite, elliptic to ovate leaves, usually smooth-margined but sometimes lobed. Flowers pink with varying amounts of white, clustered or solitary at branch ends.

Common snowberry (S. *albus*) is an erect, deciduous shrub usually 3–6 ft tall. Leaves pale green, opposite, elliptic to oval, 1–2 in long, lacking hairs on both surfaces. Stems flexible,

Common snowberry (S. *albus*)

> **WARNING:** *The branches, leaves and roots of these plants are poisonous and contain the alkaloid chelidonine, which can cause vomiting, diarrhea, depression and sedation.*

Mountain snowberry (*S. oreophilus*)

Desert snowberry (*S. longiflorus*)

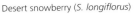

strong, gray, bark becoming shredded on more mature specimens. Flowers pink to white, broadly funnel-shaped, ¼ in long, in small clusters at stem tips. Tough, dense, underground root system (rhizomes) spreads rapidly, quickly forming an impenetrable thicket if left alone. Grows throughout our area on rocky banks, in hedgerows and along forest edges and roadsides.

Desert snowberry (*S. longiflorus*) is a small shrub less than 4 ft tall, with stiff, red-barked branches frequently covered with spines and minute hairs. Leaves opposite, less than 1 in long. Flowers whitish pink, with long, narrow tubes and spreading petals. Limited in our area to southeastern Oregon.

Mountain snowberry (*S. oreophilus*) is similar to common snowberry but is found in the mountains of eastern Washington and Oregon. It is a branching shrub that reaches 4 ft in height.

Roundleaf snowberry (*S. rotundifolius*) is a small, stiff shrub 2–4 ft tall. Bark becomes shredded with age. Leaves much wider and rounder than other snowberries, paler and more prominently veined on the underside. Flowers pink, bell-shaped, about twice as long as wide. Found in eastern Oregon.

Trailing snowberry (*S. hesperius*) is a trailing shrub that never attains a height of more than 18 in but can reach 9 ft in length. Stem often hairy, rooting at nodes. Leaves opposite, elliptic, ½–1 in long, smooth-margined or with a few shallow lobes, upper surface smooth, underside hairy. Flowers pink. Found on both slopes of the Cascade, Olympic and Coastal ranges, usually near water. Also called: creeping snowberry • *S. mollis* ssp. *hesperius*.

Western snowberry (*S. occidentalis*) is also similar to common snowberry but is shorter (1–3 ft tall) with twigs that are usually hairy and leaves that are hairy on the underside. Found on prairies, floodplains and along forest edges at low to middle elevations on both sides of the Cascades in Washington. Also called: wolfberry.

Western snowberry (*S. occidentalis*)

Trailing snowberry (*S. hesperius*)

227

Climbing Nightshade *Solanum dulcamara*

Also called: bittersweet nightshade

Climbing nightshade (*S. dulcamara*)

Climbing nightshade is native to Eurasia and was introduced into our area prior to the late 1860s, at which time the berries were used by the Makah to treat stomach issues. An infusion of the crushed stems can be used to treat chronic eczema and skin abrasions. The berries are widely considered poisonous, and in some areas, they are responsible for more calls to the poison control center than any other berry. Solanine, a toxic alkaloid glycoside that is present in green potatoes and potato leaves is found in climbing nightshade. A study on the toxicity of climbing nightshade berries found that the unripe berries produced gastrointestinal lesions in mice. However, no lesions were observed in mice that were fed ripe berries, leading the authoring toxicologists to conclude that human ingestion of small quantities of ripe berries does not require "aggressive" treatment from poison control workers. Although other toxicologists have confirmed that the concentrations of toxic alkaloids decreases with ripening, the use of climbing nightshade berries for food is not recommended, and the ingestion of unripe berries should be reported immediately to the nearest poison control center, especially if eaten by a child.

EDIBILITY: poisonous

FRUIT: Ovoid berries ³⁄₈ in wide, slightly longer, green maturing to orange, and then finally to glossy red.

SEASON: Flowers May to September. Fruit ripens August and September.

DESCRIPTION: Herbaceous plant that tends to climb on other vegetation, arising from a perennial rhizome. Leaves alternate, long-stalked, with either 1 simple, ovate blade or a large terminal lobe with 1–2 smaller lateral lobes. Flowers purple with yellow anthers, in a many-branched inflorescence of 10–25 flowers. Grows in damp soil in clearings and thickets throughout our region.

Belladonna *Atropa bella-donna*

Also called: deadly nightshade

Belladonna (*A. bella-donna*)

All parts of the belladonna plant are considered poisonous, but the berries are most often implicated in accidental poisonings when consumed by children or eaten by adults who have mistaken them for other berries. The plant contains toxic tropane alkaloids, and consuming as few as 3 berries has been reported to be lethal to a child.

In carefully controlled dosages, these toxic berries have important medicinal uses. Belladonna has a long history of use as an herbal medicine for problems related to inflammation and stiff muscles. The alkaloids hyoscyamine, atropine and scopolamine are isolated and used in a variety of pharmaceuticals for the treatment of motion sickness and

various gastrointestinal issues, as well as by eye doctors to dilate the pupil and paralyze the ocular muscles. The name "belladonna" is Italian for "beautiful lady," and, in the past, fashion-hungry women used drops of a tincture of the plant to dilate their pupils, making their eyes appear more lustrous and seductive.

EDIBILITY: poisonous; low doses cause stomach pains, fever and disorientation, whereas high doses cause hallucinations, convulsions and death

FRUIT: Cherry-sized berries arising singly above a leafy bract on a long stalk, green and smaller when young, maturing to a glossy black.

SEASON: Flowers in summer. Fruit begins to ripen in August.

DESCRIPTION: Small, shrubby, herbaceous perennial reaching 5 ft tall. Leaves short-stalked, with pointed tips and smooth margins, alternate along the stem, frequently with pairs of 1 large leaf and 1 small leaf on the same side of the stem. Flowers tubular, purple, 1 in long or more, borne singly in leaf axils. Usually planted as an ornamental in gardens but occasionally escapes cultivation in coastal areas.

Coastal Manroot *Marah oreganus*

Coastal manroot (*M. oreganus*)

Coastal manroot is part of the cucumber family, and like most of its non-domesticated relatives, has very bitter fruit. The genus name *Marah* means "bitter" in Hebrew. Little is known about the toxicity of this plant, but a man was poisoned in Oregon in 1986 when he consumed the seeds (for unknown reasons). Coastal manroot has enormous roots that can be as wide as a Frisbee and as long as a leg. Sadly, they are not edible. Considered poisonous by many Native Americans in our area, the roots were sometimes used as an eyewash, a poultice for rheumatism or a fish poison. The heavy vines are often problematic weeds in agricultural fields.

EDIBILITY: not recommended; extremely bitter, with a documented fatal case of poisoning from consumption of the seeds

FRUIT: Spiny, green, cucumber-like fruits, 1–3 in long, with large seeds.

SEASON: Flowers April to June. Fruit ripens throughout summer.

DESCRIPTION: Perennial, non-woody vine arising from a large, woody root. Stems grow anew each spring and climb using branched tendrils. Leaves alternate, to 8 in long, with broad, triangular lobes. Flowers white, usually 5 spreading lobes (sometimes more). Found west of the Cascades at low elevations in fields, fencerows, thickets and open areas.

Red Baneberry *Actaea rubra*

Also called: snake berry • *A. arguta, A. eburnea*

Red baneberry (*A. rubra*)

Baneberry is related to the commercial phytomedicine black cohosh (*A. racemosa*), and some indigenous peoples used baneberry root tea in a similar way to treat menstrual and postpartum problems, as well as colds, coughs, rheumatism and syphilis. Herbalists have used baneberry roots as a strong anti-spasmodic, anti-inflammatory, vasodilator and sedative, usually for treating menstrual cramps and menopausal discomforts.

Baneberry is a striking-looking plant with its attractive foliage and delicate stems of puffy, white flowers in spring, followed by showy spikes of red or white berries in the fall. Planted with ferns, hostas and other shade-loving species, it makes a decorative addition to a shade garden.

EDIBILITY: poisonous

FRUIT: Glossy, red or white berries, 1/4–1/2 in wide, very showy, several-seeded, singly on long stalks.

SEASON: Flowers May to July. Fruit ripens July to August.

DESCRIPTION: Branched, leafy, generally solitary perennial herb, 1–3 ft tall, from a woody stem-base and fibrous roots. Stems long, wiry. Leaves alternate, coarsely toothed, few and large, divided 2–3 times into threes, crowded at base of stem, sparser near the top of the plant. Flowers white, 5–10 slender petals each 1/8 in long, in long-stalked, rounded, many-flowered clusters. Inhabits deciduous forests, mixed coniferous forests, subalpine meadows, moist woodlands, streambanks and swamps at low to montane elevations.

WARNING: *All parts of baneberry are poisonous, but the roots and berries are the most toxic. Indeed, the common name "baneberry" is derived from the Anglo-Saxon* bana, *which means "murderous." Eating as few as 2 to 6 berries can cause severe cramps and burning in the stomach, vomiting, bloody diarrhea, increased pulse, headaches and/or dizziness. Severe poisoning results in convulsions, paralysis of the respiratory system and cardiac arrest. No deaths have been reported in North America, probably because the berries are extremely bitter and unpleasant to eat.*

Pokeweed *Phytolacca americana*

Pokeweed (*P. americaca*)

Pokeweed is a poisonous plant that, when properly prepared, has some edible parts. Several types of toxic saponins are concentrated in the roots and seeds, but all parts should be regarded with caution. A mitogenic protein lectin is another class of toxin found in pokeweed and can cause blood cell abnormalities. It can be absorbed by simply handling the plant or through ingestion. Pokeweed is included here among other poisonous plants because we haven't personally eaten it and there is little scientific evidence about the effect of cooking on the known toxins. The young greens and shoots, as well as the mature fruit, are eaten in many parts of the southeastern U.S. after repeatedly boiling the greens and shoots, or cooking and straining the seeds from the berries. The significance of pokeweed salad to Southerners is captured in the 1969 song "Polk Salad Annie," which was covered by Elvis Presley.

The genus name *Phytolacca* is Greek, meaning "red dye plant" and refers to the red-staining fruit of many members of this genus. The etymology of the common name is less clear as "poke" can refer to a number of things including a bag (perhaps for harvesting greens and berries?) or the shape of the inflorescence, which somewhat resembles a fire poker.

EDIBILITY: roots and seeds poisonous, young greens and mature fruit pulp reportedly edible after careful preparation

FRUIT: Berries green maturing to black, ¼–½ in wide, numerous in red-stemmed clusters up to 8 in long.

SEASON: Flowers June to August. Fruit ripens July to September.

DESCRIPTION: A perennial herb reaching 10 ft tall. Leaves alternate, to 14 in long and 7 in wide, on stalks ½–2 in long. Flowers can be many colors including white, greenish white, pink or purple, arranged in racemes 2–6 in long. Uncommon and scattered, found mainly west of the Cascades.

Spurgelaurel   *Daphne laureola*

Also called: laurel-leaved daphne

Spurgelaurel (*Daphne laureola*)

Spurgelaurel is native to Eurasia and was introduced fairly recently to western Washington (possibly soon after the year 2000), where it has quickly invaded Douglas-fir forests and is now classified as a Class B noxious weed. All parts of the plant are poisonous to humans, but birds eat the berries and are probably an important vector for dispersal.

Spurgelaurel is very shade tolerant and can form dense stands in Garry oak woodlands, Douglas-fir forests and likely other ecosystems. Restoration workers engaged in pulling spurgelaurel occasionally develop rashes from contact with the sap, and gloves are recommended for anyone handling the plant.

No members of the *Daphne* genus are native to North America, and all have poisonous fruit. These species are planted ornamentally for their fragrant, sometimes exceptionally early blossoming flowers and colorful fruit. In Nepal, the inner bark of 2 related species called lokta (*D. papyracea* and sometimes *D. bhoula*) are made into paper for official and artisanal use. Perhaps an enterprising person could produce paper from our invasive spurgelaurel because the bark separates with the same ease as lokta bark.

EDIBILITY: all parts poisonous; sap known to cause skin rashes

FRUIT: Egg-shaped drupes ⅜–½ in long, green maturing to black, one-seeded, in clusters along stems.

SEASON: Flowers in late winter and early spring. Usually fruits by late spring.

DESCRIPTION: Evergreen shrub 1½–5 ft tall, usually with an upright growth habit and few branches. Young stems green, bark maturing to gray with a yellowish cast. Stems very flexible. Leaves 2–5 in long, ½–1 in wide, smooth-margined, dark green upper surface, paler underside, arranged in spirals on the stem, usually in dense whorls near the ends of shoots. Flowers tubular, yellow-green, clustered along the stem next to and obscured by the leaves. Highly problematic in western Washington

and increasingly common throughout our area.

Mistletoes & Dwarf Mistletoes
Phoradendron spp. and *Arceuthobium* spp.

Juniper mistletoe (*P. juniperinum*)

Mistletoes are a diverse group of hemiparasitic plants—parasites that are still capable of producing their own food with their evergreen leaves. They attach to a variety of host trees and rely on the trees for water and minerals. Dwarf mistletoes, also hemiparasitic, actively synthesize sunlight to make plant tissue as seedlings, but as mature plants, they parasitize their hosts more intensively and rely only lightly on photosynthesis.

Mistletoes reproduce with the aid of birds, which eat the berries and may defecate the sticky seeds onto the branches of other host trees. The name "mistletoe" is likely derived from this phenomenon, *mistel* being the Anglo-Saxon word for "dung" and *tan* the Anglo-Saxon word for "branch."

However, in our area, the berries are usually eaten by cedar waxwings, which do not pass the seeds through their gut but instead use their bills to wipe them onto branches. Dwarf mistletoes produce berries that explosively expel their sticky seeds at speeds up to 50 mph!

Mistletoe is commonly used as a Christmas decoration. It is often hung in the house to protect it from lightning or fire until it is replaced the following year. As the tradition goes, young men may kiss girls under the mistletoe, but must remove a berry each time they do. When all the berries are gone, the privilege ceases.

EDIBILITY: all parts poisonous (see Warning)

FRUIT: Mistletoes have translucent, white, yellow, orange, pink or red berries with sticky seeds. Dwarf mistletoes have greenish to bluish fruit.

SEASON: Flowers in spring and summer. Fruit ripens in late summer and fall.

DESCRIPTION: Mistletoes are small, spherical, epiphytic shrubs that have opposite, leathery, green leaves 1–2 in long, with smooth margins. They grow on both conifers and hardwoods. Dwarf mistletoes are smaller and lack well-developed green leaves. They grow exclusively on conifers. Among our 4 species of mistletoe and 9 species of dwarf mistletoe, many are often host specific and therefore easily identified by the tree in which they grow.

Dense mistletoe (*P. densum*) is a densely branched, hemiparastic shrub

similar to juniper mistletoe, with branches 12–18 in long and green leaves about ½ in long and wide. Berries yellowish or pale pink. Grows on junipers (*Juniperus* spp.). Also called: *P. bolleanum.*

Incense cedar mistletoe (*P. libocedri*) is a small, hanging or upright shrub that grows on incense cedar (*Calocedrus decurrens*). Berries light pink or yellow. Lumped by some botanists with juniper mistletoe.

Juniper mistletoe (*P. juniperinum*) is a densely branched, yellowish green, hemiparastic shrub with branches 8–16 in long that come together in a woody base. Berries smooth, $^3/_{16}$ in wide, maturing from green to pink-white in September. Grows on junipers (*Juniperus* spp.) in Oregon. Reportedly edible.

Pacific mistletoe (*P. villosum*) is a large, bushy, hemiparasitic shrub with grayish green or yellowish green, hairy branches. Leaves to 2 in long. Berries pale pink, maturing in the fall. Found in Oregon mostly on Garry oak (*Quercus garryana*), smooth sumac (*Rhus glabra*) and madrona (*Arbutus menziesii*).

Pacific mistletoe (*P. villosum*)

American dwarf mistletoe (*A. americanum*) is similar to western dwarf mistletoe but is a very small (1–3 in tall), yellowish green, hemiparastic shrub growing on pines, usually lodgepole pine (*Pinus contorta*). Accessory branches (if any) in one plane. Flowers April to May. Fruits ripen to a blue-green color in August and September. Mostly found east of the Cascade Crest.

Douglas-fir dwarf mistletoe (*A. douglasii*) is similar to fir dwarf mistletoe but is usually less than 1 in tall and grows exclusively on the branches of Douglas-fir (*Pseudotsuga menziesii*). Stems greenish or bluish green with fan-like accessory branches. Berries ripen in September and October. Found mostly east of the Cascade Crest with a few occurrences in Josephine and Jackson Counties in southwestern Oregon.

Fir dwarf mistletoe (*A. abietinum*) is a small, yellowish, hemiparasitic shrub with scaly, yellowish stems and grows mostly on firs (*Abies* spp.). Accessory branches whorled. Flowers whitish yellow. Blooms May to July and produces

Fir dwarf mistletoe (*A. abietinum*)

very small, white berries from August to December. Found at low to moderate elevations on both side of the Cascades.

Hemlock dwarf mistletoe (*A. tsugense*) is a hemisparasitic shrub similar to fir dwarf mistletoe and is found in hemlocks (*Tsuga* spp.). Flowers whitish yellow. Blooms May to July and produces very small, white berries from August to December. Lumped by some botanists with western dwarf mistletoe.

Knobcone pine dwarf mistletoe (*A. siskiyouense*) is similar to western dwarf mistletoe but is a small, brownish shrub found only on knobcone pine (*Pinus attenuata*) in the Klamath Mountains of southern Oregon and northern California. Flowers whitish yellow. Blooms May to July and produces very small, white berries from August to December. Lumped by some botanists with western dwarf mistletoe.

Larch dwarf mistletoe (*A. laricis*) is a hemiparasitic shrub similar to fir dwarf mistletoe and is found in larches (*Larix* spp.).

Limber dwarf mistletoe (*A. cyanocarpum*) is similar to western dwarf mistletoe but is usually less than 1 in tall, with greenish brown stems. Grows on limber pine (*Pinus flexilis*) and whitebark pine (*Pinus albicaulis*) in the mountains of central Oregon. Flowers whitish yellow. Blooms May to July and produces very small, white berries from August to December. Lumped by some botanists with western dwarf mistletoe.

Pacific mistletoe (*P. villosum*)

Western dwarf mistletoe (*A. campylo-podum*) is a small shrub, 1–6 in tall, with orangey yellow to brownish, many-branching stems. Flowers whitish yellow. Blooms May to July and produces very small, white berries from August to December. Grows on lodgepole pine (*Pinus contorta*) and ponderosa pine (*Pinus ponderosa*) from sea level to middle elevations on both sides of the Cascades.

Western white pine dwarf mistletoe (*A. monticola*) is similar to western dwarf mistletoe but is a reddish to brownish shrub found only on western white pine (*Pinus monticola*) in the Klamath Mountains of southern Oregon. Flowers whitish yellow. Blooms May to July and produces very small, white berries from August to December. Lumped by some botanists with western dwarf mistletoe.

Western dwarf mistletoe (*A. campylopodum*)

WARNING: *All parts of mistletoes and dwarf mistletoes are poison and contain toxic lectins that inhibit protein systhesis. Eating just a few berries can cause diarrhea, and gastric distress increases with higher doses. The sole exception in our area is juniper mistletoe, which produces berries that were eaten as a starvation food by Native Americans.*

Privet   *Ligustrum vulgare*

Privet (*L. vulgare*)

Privet is often planted in hedgerows and some suggest that the common name is derived from the word "private." The species name *vulgare* means "common," since this plant is found throughout much of Eurasia. An escaped ornamental, privet is increasingly common in disturbed sites in urban areas and along forest edges, and it can be difficult to remove. Robins and other thrushes eat the berries and disperse the seeds, but the fruit is mildly toxic to humans. Symptoms of privet poisoning include headaches, weakness, low blood pressure, vomiting and diarrhea.

The fruit tastes terrible, so there isn't much danger of being poisoned.

EDIBILITY: all parts poisonous

FRUIT: Glossy, black, round berries $^3/_{16}$–$^1/_4$ in wide.

SEASON: Flowers April to June. Fruit ripens in late summer and persists through winter.

DESCRIPTION: Perennial, semi-evergreen shrub 4–10 ft tall. Stems upright to spreading. Bark grayish brown. Leaves opposite, oval-lance-shaped, shiny, smooth-margined. Flowers white, 4-petaled, in long, many-branched clusters (panicles). Found in low-elevation woodlands, along forest edges and in disturbed areas west of the Cascades.

Glossary

accessory fruit: a fruit that develops from the thickened calyx of the flower rather than from the ovary (e.g., soapberry)

achene: a small, dry fruit that doesn't split open; often seed-like in appearance; distinguished from a nutlet by its relatively thin wall

acuminate: tapering to a sharp point

alkaloid: any of a group of bitter-tasting, usually mildly alkaline plant chemicals; many alkaloids affect the nervous system and can be toxic

alternate: situated singly at each node or joint (e.g., leaves on a stem) or regularly between other organs (e.g., stamens alternating with petals)

anaphylaxis: a severe allergic reaction to a foreign substance (e.g., the venom in a bee sting) to which the body has become sensitized, typically from previous exposure

annual: a plant that completes its life cycle in one growing season

anther: the pollen-producing sac of a stamen

anthraquinone: an organic compound found in some plants that has a laxative effect when ingested; also used commercially as a dye and in the pulp and paper industry

aril: a specialized cover attached to a mature seed, usually brightly colored and fleshy

armed: having thorns, spines or bristles

axil: the angle between a side organ (e.g., a leaf) and the part to which it is attached (e.g., a stem)

berry: a fleshy, simple fruit that contains one or more ovule-bearing structures (carpels), each containing one or more seeds; the outside covering (endocarp) of a berry is generally soft, moist and fleshy (e.g., a blueberry)

Vascular Plant Parts

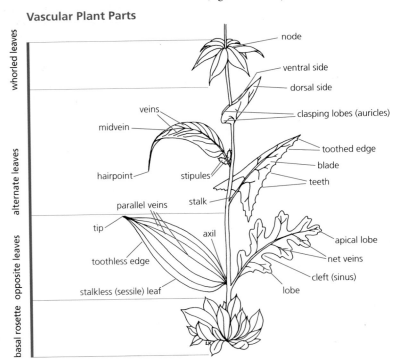

biennial: a plant that completes its life cycle in two years, usually producing flowers and seeds in the second year

bitters: an alcoholic preparation, typically consumed with a meal, that contains bitter herbs to aid digestion

bog: a peat-covered wetland characterized by *Sphagnum* mosses, heath shrubs and sometimes trees (most often black spruce)

bract: a specialized leaf below a flower or associated with a flower cluster

calcareous: having a high calcium content

calyx: the outer (lowermost) circle of floral parts, usually green and leaf-like; composed of separate or fused lobes called sepals

carpel: a fertile leaf bearing undeveloped seed(s); one or more carpels join together to form a pistil

cathartic: a substance that purges the bowels

compound leaf: a leaf composed of two or more leaflets

compound drupe: a collection of tiny fruits that form within the same flower from individual ovaries; often crunchy and seedy (e.g., a boysenberry)

cone: a fruit made up of scales (sporophylls) arranged in a spiral or overlapping pattern around a central core and in which the seeds develop between the scales (e.g., juniper "berries")

corolla: the second circle of floral parts, composed of separate or fused segments called petals; usually conspicuous in size and color but can be small or absent

cultivar: a plant or animal variety originating from cultivation

deciduous: having structures (typically leaves, petals or seeds) that are shed at maturity and in autumn

drupe: a fruit with an outer fleshy part covered by a thin skin and surrounding a hard or bony stone that encloses a single seed (e.g., a plum)

drupelet: a tiny drupe; part of an aggregate fruit such as a raspberry

edible with caution: berries that are palatable but have differing reports about their edibility; perhaps only toxic if ingested in large amounts or if unripe or not properly prepared

emetic: a substance that induces vomiting

endocarp: the inner layer of the pericarp

eulachon grease: grease from the eulachon (*Thaleichthys pacificus*), a small species of fish in the smelt family that lives most of its life in the Pacific Ocean but comes inland to fresh water to spawn

fruit: a ripened ovary, together with any other structures that ripen with it as a unit

glabrous: hairless, smooth

glandular: having glands, which are small, sometimes hair-like structures that give off a sticky substance and may be present on various parts of a plant

glaucous: having a frosted appearance owing to a whitish powdery or waxy coating

globose: round, spherical

glycoside: a two-parted molecule composed of a sugar and an aglycone, usually becoming poisonous when digested and the sugar is separated from the poisonous aglycone

habitat: the environment in which a plant or animal is normally found

haw: the fruit of a hawthorn, usually with a fleshy outer layer enclosing many dry seeds

heath: a member of the heath family (Ericaceae)

herbaceous: a plant or plant part lacking woody tissues

hip: a fruit composed of a collection of bony seeds (achenes), each of which comes from a single pistil, covered by a fleshy receptacle that is contracted at the mouth (e.g., a rose hip)

hybrid: a cross between two species

hypanthium: a ring or cup around the ovary formed by fused parts of the petals, sepals and/or stamens

inflorescence: a flower cluster

involucre: a set of bracts encircling and immediately below a flower cluster

lanceolate: widest at the middle and pointed at the tip

lenticel: a slightly raised pore on the bark of a root, trunk or branch

mesic: habitat with intermediate moisture levels, neither very dry nor very moist

montane: mountainous habitat below timberline

multiple fruit: a dense cluster of small fruits, each produced by an individual flower (e.g., a mulberry)

node: the place where a leaf or branch is attached to a stem; a joint

nutlet: a small, hard, dry, one-seeded fruit or part of a fruit; does not split open

opposite: situated across from each other at the same node (e.g., leaves) or situated directly in front of one another (e.g., stamens opposite petals); not alternate or whorled

ovary: the organ at the base of the pistil that contains undeveloped seeds; matures to become all or part of the fruit after fertilization

ovule: an organ that develops into a seed after fertilization

palmate: divided into three or more lobes or leaflets diverging from a common point, like fingers on a hand

peduncle: the stem of a flower or fruit

pemmican: a traditional Native American food made from finely pounded dried meat, fat and sometimes dried fruit

perennial: a plant that lives for three or more years, usually flowering and fruiting for several years

pericarp: the part of a fruit that derives from the ovary wall; generally consists of three layers: endocarp, mesocarp and exocarp (from inside to outside)

petal: a unit of the corolla; usually white or brightly colored to attract insects

petiole: a leaf stalk

phytomedicine: the use of plants as medicine

pinnate: with branches, lobes, leaflets or veins arranged on both sides of a central stalk or vein; feather-like

pistil: the female part of the flower, composed of the stigma, style and ovary

pitch: a sticky or gummy substance produced by trees

poisonous: a substance that is unsafe to ingest because it can cause serious harm, including injury, illness or death

pome: a fleshy fruit with a core (e.g., an apple), comprised of an enlarged hypanthium around a compound ovary

prostrate: growing flat along the ground

pseudocarp: a simple fruit with flesh that derives from a part other than the ovary (e.g., a strawberry)

purgative: causing watery evacuation of the bowels (diarrhea)

raceme: an unbranched cluster of stalked flowers on a common, elongated central stalk, blooming from the bottom up

receptacle: an expanded stalk tip at the center of a flower bearing the floral organs or the small, crowded flowers of a head

recurved: curved under (usually referring to leaf margins)

reflexed: bent backward or downward

rhizomatous: having rhizomes

rhizome: an underground, often lengthened stem; distinguished from the root by the presence of nodes and buds or scale-like leaves

saponin: any of a group of plant glycosides that form a soapy lather when agitated; causes diarrhea and vomiting when ingested but used commercially in detergents

sepal: one segment of the calyx; usually green and leaf-like

species: a group of closely related plants or animals; ranked below genus and above subspecies and variety in biological classification

spore: a reproductive body composed of one or several cells that is capable of asexual reproduction (i.e., does not require fertilization)

sporophyll: a spore-bearing leaf; a scale of a conifer cone

spp.: the abbreviation of "species" (plural)

spur: a hollow appendage on a petal or sepal, usually functioning as a nectary

spur-shoot: a short branch or stem

ssp.: the abbreviation of "subspecies"

stolon: a slender, prostrate, spreading branch, rooting and often developing new shoots and/or plants at its nodes or tip

style: the part of the pistil connecting the stigma to the ovary; often elongated and stalk-like

subalpine: the region just below treeline, but above the foothills

subspecies: a naturally occurring, regional form of a species; ranked below species and above variety in biological classification

sucker: a shoot originating from a rhizome or root

tepal: a sepal or petal, when these structures are not easily distinguished from one another

throat: the opening into a corolla tube or calyx tube

toxic: a substance that can cause damage, illness or death

tundra: a habitat in which the subsoil remains frozen year-round; characterized by plants with low growth and lacking trees

unarmed: having no thorns, spines or bristles

variety: a naturally occurring variant of a species; below the level of subspecies in biological classification

whorled: arranged in a ring (e.g., leaves around a stem)

Parts of a Regular Flower

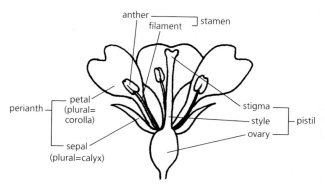

References

Chestnut, Victor. 1902. *Plants Used by the Indians of Mendocino County, California.* U.S. Government Printing Office, Washington, DC.

Derig, Betty, and Margaret Fuller. 2001. *Wild Berries of the West.* Mountain Press Publishing, Missoula MT.

Elias, Thomas, and Peter Dykeman. 1982. *Edible Wild Plants: A North American Field Guide to Over 200 Natural Foods.* Sterling Publishing, New York, NY.

Gunther, Erna. 1988. *Ethnobotany of Western Washington.* University of Washington Press, Seattle, WA.

Hamersley Chambers, Fiona. 2011. *Wild Berries of British Columbia.* Lone Pine Publishing, Vancouver, BC.

Hitchcock, C. Leo, and A. Cronquist. 1973. *Flora of the Pacific Northwest.* University of Washington Press, Seattle, WA.

Hunn, Eugene. 1990. *Nch'i-Wána, "The Big River": Mid-Columbia Indians and Their Land.* University of Washington Press, Seattle, WA.

Kindscher, Kelly. 2012. "The Ethnobotany of *Physalis longifolia*, the Longleaf Groundcherry, and related *Physalis* species of north of Mexico." 35th Annual Conference of the Society of Ethnobiology.

Kuhnlein, Harriet, and Nancy Turner. 1991. *Traditional Plant Foods of Canadian Indigenous Peoples: Nutrition, Botany, and Use.* Gordon and Breach Science Publishers, Philadelphia, PA.

Moerman, Daniel. 1998. *Native American Ethnobotany.* Timber Press, Portland, OR.

Pojar, Jim, and Andy Mackinnon 1994. *Plants of the Pacific Northwest Coast.* Lone Pine Publishing, Vancouver, BC.

Sturtevant, Edward. 1919. *Sturtevant's Notes on Edible Plants.* U.P. Hedrick, ed. J.B. Lyon Company, Albany, NY.

Thayer, Samuel. 2006. *Forager's Harvest: A Guide to Identifying, Harvesting, and Preparing Edible Wild Plants.* Forager's Harvest Press, Birchwood, WI.

Thayer, Samuel. 2010. *Nature's Garden: A Guide to Identifying, Harvesting, and Preparing Edible Wild Plants.* Forager's Harvest Press, Birchwood, WI.

Turner, Nancy, and Adam Szczawinski. 1991. *Common Poisonous Plants and Mushrooms of North America.* Timber Press, Portland, OR.

Turner, Nancy. 1995. *Food Plants of Coastal First Peoples.* Royal BC Museum, Victoria, BC.

Turner, Nancy. 1997. *Food Plants of Interior First Peoples.* Royal BC Museum, Victoria, BC.

Internet Resources

CalFlora. www.calflora.org

Efloras.org, Flora of North America. www.efloras.org/flora_page.aspx?flora_id=1

E-Flora BC, Geography Department, University of British Columbia. www.geog.ubc.ca/biodiversity/eflora

Jepson eFlora, Jepson Herbarium. ucjeps.berkeley.edu/IJM.html

Native American Ethnobotany, University of Michigan–Dearborn. herb.umd.umich.edu

Oregan Flora Project, Department of Botany and Plant Pathology, Oregon State University. www.oregonflora.org/index.php

Plants for a Future. www.pfaf.org/user/default.aspx

USDA PLANTS Database: Natural Resources Conservation Service. plants.usda.gov

Wildflowers of the Pacific Northwest. Turner Photographics. www.pnwflowers.com

WTU Herbarium, Burke Museum of Natural History and Culture, University of Washington. www.burkemuseum.org/herbarium

Index to Common and Scientific Names

Entries in **boldface** type refer to the primary species accounts.

Photo & Illustration Credits

Photo Credits: **Aconcagua** 95a; **Zoya Akulova** 99, 206, 213a; **Silvia Alba** 75a; **Björn Appel** 52a; **Drew Avery** 190; **Nino Barbieri** 244; **Lee Beavington** 13, 15, 16, 19ab, 22b, 23, 24, 26, 28, 29a, 31ac, 32, 33ab, 34, 36, 37bc, 44, 48, 49a, 50ad, 54, 55a, 72, 73, 74ab, 79a, 83, 84, 85, 87abc, 88, 90a, 91, 92, 96b, 104, 105a, 106, 110, 111ab, 112, 113ab, 116, 117, 118, 121, 122, 123, 127ab, 128ab, 131a, 136, 137bc, 140a, 150, 151, 153b, 154, 161a, 162a, 174ab, 176, 177a, 178b, 179b, 180, 182, 183a, 185a, 187b, 188a, 214, 215ab, 216, 217, 222, 223, 224, 225ab, 228, 229a, 234, 235ab; **born1945** 219ab; **BotBln** 173b; **Barry Breckling** 107, 108; **Alfred Cook** 209ab; **Dr. G. Dallas and Margaret Hanna** © **California Academy of Sciences** 172; **Dcrjsr (Jane Shelby Richardson)** 105b; **Joe DiTomaso** 195b; **Lee Dittmann** 226a; **D. Eickhoff** 201b; **Tom Engstrom** 159b; **Robert Flogaust** 65; **Franco Folini** 233ab; **Wouter Hagens** 159a; **Eric Hunt** 220; **Karel Jakubec** 231b; **Neil Jennings** 69, 90b; **Norman Jensen** 101b; **Krista Kagume** 70, 183b; **Makoto Kanda** 81a; **Dean Kelch** 198a; **Linda Kershaw** 18, 39b, 46, 67c, 79b, 95b, 145, 147, 177b, 178a, 184, 185c, 187a, 189; **Sangeet Khalsa** 242; **Brian Klinkenberg** 135b; **Don Knoke** 142a, 143c, 192, 194a, 195a; **Neal Kramer** 50c, 196a, 199b, 201a; **Louis Landry** 194b; **Matt Lavin** 160; **T. Abe Lloyd** 31b, 29b, 30, 37a, 40b, 41, 43a, 45a, 47, 49b, 52b, 55b, 57ab, 58, 59a, 60, 61, 62, 63ab, 64, 66, 67b, 71a, 80b, 94ac, 96a, 114, 115, 119, 125b, 126a, 130, 137a, 146, 149ab, 152, 153a, 155ab, 156b, 157b, 158, 162b, 165, 167a, 169b, 202, 203ab, 245ab; **Ron Long** 166; **Steve Matson** 209c, 226b; **Jean-Jacques Milan** 157a; **Jason Matthias Mills** 175b; **Gernot Molitor** 239a; **Keir Morse** 50b, 93, 102b, 109, 140b, 141, 142b, 168, 169a, 193, 199a, 204, 205, 208, 210, 212, 227ab, 241, 243ab; **Daniel Mosquin** 232; **National Park Service** 175a; **Neelix** 53; **Nimmolo** 171ab; **Jessica O'Brien** 211; **OlafE** 75b; **Richard Old** 52c; **Paolo** 191b; **Pascal** 229b; **Pixeltoo** 239b; **Sten Porse** 131b; **Robert Potts** © **California Academy of Sciences** 196b; **Sandy R** 173a; **Jim Riley** 95c; **Stan Shebs** 89, 191a; **John Shortland** 238; **Walter Siegmund** 76b; **Tomasz Sienicki** 59b; **Sigma64** 179a; **Simonjoan** 76a; **Robert Sivinski** 240; **Virginia Skilton** 14, 22a, 71b, 98, 135a, 213b, 218, 221; **Forest and Kim Starr** 197; **Stickpen** 200; **Hedwig Storch** 161b; **Super cyclist** 56; **SuperiorNF** 207; **Mr Tonreg** 163c; **Mark Turner** 39a, 43bc, 67a, 80a, 97c, 103ab, 143ab, 163ab, 170; **Robert D. Turner and Nancy J. Turner** 10, 11, 17, 25, 27, 35, 38, 51, 68, 78, 82, 86, 94b, 97ab, 100ab, 101a, 103c, 120ab, 125a, 126b, 132, 133, 138, 144, 156a, 164ab, 181, 186, 188b; **VoDeTan2Dericks-Tan** 167b; **Doug Waylett** 198b; **Charles Webber** © **California Academy of Sciences** 45b, 102a, 185b; **Fred Weinmann** 81b; **Bri Weldon** 148; **Michael Wolf** 40a; **H. Zell** 230, 231a, 236, 237.

Illustration Credits: **Frank Burman** 30, 33, 35, 43, 49, 51, 55, 58b, 66, 69, 76ab, 79, 81, 82abc, 83, 87, 89ab, 90b, 95, 96, 97, 112ab, 117, 120, 122, 124, 129, 130, 133ab, 134ab, 135, 141, 145, 146, 152, 154, 173, 178, 179b, 180, 183ab, 187, 189, 191, 206, 209, 210, 215, 217b, 221ab, 223, 233, 237; **Linda Kershaw** 148, 244; **George Penetrante** 193; **Ian Sheldon** 36, 41, 42ab, 44, 46, 47, 54, 57, 58a, 61, 62ab, 67, 85ab, 90a, 107, 111, 113ab, 115, 119, 139, 147, 151, 153ab, 179a, 188, 217a, 219ab, 225ab, 235.

About the Authors

© Vicki Pallan Photography

T. ABE LLOYD is an ethnobotanist and the founding director of Salal, the Cascadian Food Institute (www.cascadianfood.net), where he consults with regional Native American tribal organizations to study and promote indigenous foods. He teaches university courses in natural history and ethnobotany at Western Washington University and Whatcom Community College, as well as hands-on foraging courses at Royal Roads University.

A sixth-generation resident of the Pacific Northwest, Abe was enchanted by nature's edible bounty at a young age. In college, he enrolled in as many botany courses as he could while completing a Bachelor of Science in Natural Resource Management in 2002. Abe traveled to Nepal with the Peace Corps in 2003–04, where he volunteered for Langtang National Park conducting botanical and ethnobotanical research. He completed a Master's of Science degree in Ethnobotany at the University of Victoria in 2011 under Northwest Coast ethnoecologist Dr. Nancy J. Turner and the traditional mentorship of Kwaxsistalla clan chief, Adam Dick. Beyond his work with Salal, Abe is vice president of the Koma Kulshan Chapter of the Washington Native Plant Society, an active member of the Northwest Mushroomers' Association and a former board member of the Society of Ethnobiology. An avid forager, Abe collects more than half of all he eats.

FIONA HAMERSLEY CHAMBERS was born in Vancouver and spent most of her formative years living in the remote Ditidaht village site of Clo-oose, the UK countryside and the Coast Salish community of Penelakut. It is to this early experience in nature and with First Nations communities that she attributes her lifelong interest in ethnobotany, and particularly in wild foods. She holds an undergraduate degree in Environmental Studies and French from the University of Victoria, an MSc in Environmental Change and Management from Oxford University, and a masters degree in Environmental Design from the University of Calgary. Her current PhD research, under the supervision of renowned ethnoecologist Dr. Nancy Turner, is investigating how North-west Coast First Nations traditionally managed their extensive berry resources. Fiona is multilingual, has travelled widely and maintains a strong interest in learning about traditional plant uses wherever she goes. She has taught at the School of Environmental Studies at the University of Victoria since 1999, as well as at Pacific Rim College and the Bamfield Marine Sciences Centre. She also escapes to work as a naturalist and deckhand on the tall ship *Maple Leaf*. Fiona is the owner-operator of a successful organic farm and seed company (www.metchosinfarm.ca) and tries to keep up with two energetic boys who also love plants, bugs and foraging for wild foods, especially berries!